Basketball Coaches' Guide:

Preparing for Special Situations

by Herb Brown
with Dale Ratermann

MASTERS PRESS

NTC/Contemporary Publishing Group

Library of Congress Cataloging-in-Publication Data

Brown, Herb, 1936–
    Basketball coaches' guide: preparing for special situations / Herb Brown
and Larry Brown.
        p.   cm.
      ISBN 1-57028-095-9
      1. Basketball—Coaching.   2. Basketball—Training.   I. Ratermann,
Dale, 1956–   .   II. Title.
    GV885.3.B755   1997
    796.323'07'7—dc21   97-7511
                                                                       CIP

A Masters Press Book
Published by Contemporary Books
A division of NTC/Contemporary Publishing Group, Inc.
4255 West Touhy Avenue, Lincolnwood (Chicago), Illinois 60712-1975 U.S.A.
Printed in the United States of America
International Standard Book Number: 1-57028-095-9
00 01 02 03 04 05 RCP 20 19 18 17 16 15 14 13 12 11 10 9 8 7 6 5 4 3

Acknowledgments

I would like to thank everyone who has coached with me, played for me, mentored me or has worked with and supported my programs through the years. Each player, coach, team administrator, trainer, equipment manager and team physician has added to my enjoyment and understanding of the game of basketball. I would also like to thank my many coaching colleagues who have assisted me with their suggestions for this book.

I would especially like to thank Herb Simon and Mel Simon, owners of the Indiana Pacers, and Donnie Walsh, president of the Pacers for providing me with a forum to share my experiences. In addition, I would like to thank Tom Bast, Holly Kondras and Kim Heusel at Masters Press for their editorial assistance, and Frank McGrath for the many fine photographs.

Credits

Cover Photos©Frank McGrath

Inside Photos©Frank McGrath

Cover Design by Christy Pierce

Edited by Kim Heusel

Text Layout by Kim Heusel

Diagram Reproduction by Jason Coats, Debra Delk, Terry Varvel

Table of Contents

Symbols Used in the Diagrams xii

Coaching Philosophy 1

Communication 11

Making a Checklist 15

Teaching Your System and Philosophy 23

Practice Philosophy 25

Methods of Teaching
    and Conducting Practices 33

Defensive Principles 39

Team Defenses 73

Philosophy of Trapping
    and Double-Teaming Principles 95

Offensive Principles 107

Building an Offense 113

Types of Offensive Sets 117

Fast-Break Principles 129

Transition Principles 153

Offensive Drills 159

Screening and Cutting 165

Individual Offense 169

Rebounding 175

Incorporating Post Play 179

Combating Special Defensive Techniques 189

Special Situations 197

Game Preparations 209

Summary 215

Glossary of Key Terms 219

Foreword

Anyone aspiring to become a better coach should read this book. The material covered is essential for a coach on any level, from high school to the pros. My brother, Herb Brown, has had extensive experience and success as a coach in college, at the international level, and in the Continental Basketball Association and National Basketball Association.

This isn't a book about offense; it isn't a book about defense. It's a book about basketball and is full of ways to improve as a coach or player.

Every coach learns from the people around him. The only way you can be successful is to formulate your ideas from the players and coaches you come in contact with. Herb has coached some great players and has been associated with many fine coaches. He's never stopped being a student of the game.

My background in basketball is similar in some areas and different in others. The end result is that we both love the game. We also aren't afraid of hard work, and we're both dedicated to making each player better. You should always try to put players in a position where they can be successful. With their success comes your success.

You must feel good about everyone you work with. Every coach should love what he is doing, and Herb's passion for the game is evident in this book.

Larry Brown, Head Coach, Philadelphia 76ers

Introduction

Herb Brown has had coaching success at nearly every level of basketball. He's been a head coach in the National Basketball Association, the top professional league in Spain, the Continental Basketball Association and a major college.

He didn't achieve that success by accident. He achieved it with hard work and an analytical approach to the game.

Herb graciously is sharing much of the knowledge he has gleaned from his vast experiences. This collection is an excellent basketball primer for a novice coach, a seasoned veteran or an aspiring player at any level. It includes plenty of helpful X's and O's, but it also includes important information for off-court duties, too.

Reading and studying this book will maximize your potential as a coach and the potential of your players. If you are serious about the game and serious about success, then this book should be at the top of your reading list.

Donnie Walsh, President, Indiana Pacers

Preface

The idea for this book evolved when I realized while reviewing postgame notes that certain situations arose which we had failed to properly emphasize in our practices throughout the season.

Even after many years in the profession, it's easy to take for granted and lose sight of the changing nature and unique intricacies of the game. We all can use a "refresher course" now and then to stimulate our continued growth as coaches. After examining our material, I felt compelled to put my thoughts on paper and share these ideas with fellow coaches.

Dale and I hope this book appeals to coaches at all levels, and both men and women. After all, no matter what level your team is on, we all strive to win championships. Above all else, we should teach those we are coaching how to become better basketball players.

Herb Brown

Symbols Used in the Diagrams

1 .... Point Guard

2 .... Shooting Guard

3 .... Small Forward

4 .... Power Forward

5 .... Center

◯   Player with the Ball

=   Handoff

- - - - - - - - - →   Direction of Pass

———————————→   Direction of Player's Movement

ᐱᐯᐱᐯ→   Dribble

——————————⊣   Screen

OR   Player has the option of doing one or the other.

Coaching

Philosophy

Each coach needs to develop his own philosophy. He must decide how he wants his team to play and then implement this style. The team not only needs a system, but it must also establish an attitude! The coach should feel comfortable with the system, and in order for the team to reach its full potential, he must ensure that the team is comfortable with the system and style. No coach can truly succeed unless the system is an extension of his personality. He must work every day promoting the system to his players.

Whatever style you choose, you have to recognize that your offense must be tailored to take advantage of what the defense gives and to make the most of your players' abilities. You must teach your players how to execute effectively against all types of defensive strategies. You must also concentrate on, and not neglect, teaching sound defense yourself. Don't lose sight of the fact that you must outscore your opponents to win games and that offense coupled with strong defense wins championships.

How does a coach decide on a system? Possibly by watching other coaches' teams play, going on what he or she learned as a player, by attending clinics, working in camps or by any combination of these things. It all reverts back to what you are comfortable with and what you and your staff teach with confidence and knowledge.

You must be willing to adjust your system to your personnel. Try to take from each clinic, seminar or conference something you feel is suitable and will fit the needs of your system and your method of teaching and coaching. But don't simply copy other coaches — be yourself!

Choosing Your Style

What style of basketball do you want your team to play? Do you want to be a running team and a full-court up-tempo team playing pressure defense, or a half-court team that uses the clock and only takes good shots? Do you want to give your players some freedom or do you want to control everything from the bench? If you decide to play pressure full-court defense, forcing the action by making the other team play a fast tempo, you may not be able to orchestrate every move on the floor. Try to be flexible and utilize the individual abilities and strengths of your players. Regardless of the style you choose, be a teacher, one who works on fundamentals as well as game situations on a daily basis. Practice sets the tone for the type of coach you want to be and the product you put on the floor.

In order to answer these questions and come up with your own system, you must be realistic. If you feel that you don't have a team that is capable of pressing full court, recognize and adjust to what it can do and then decide what that team is realistically capable of accomplishing. Your goals should include, and you should emphasize, trying to make your players achieve at a level that they, or others, don't think they can attain. If you don't think your team is quick enough to press intensely, always looking to trap and steal, you still can apply full-court pressure on the inbounds pass, trap once and then drop back. Or you can wait until the opposition reaches half court to apply a trapping defense, thus cutting down the size of the court so your lack of team quickness isn't as critical a factor. Regardless of the level of your players, you must recognize their abilities and then maximize those abilities if you want them to be successful.

It is important to design drills that enable your players to both learn the system and help them adapt instinctively to changes that may occur in a game. They must be trained to react spontaneously, confidently and instinctively to every situation.

Keep the system basic and simple. Don't get too complex by trying to overcoach.

A lot of coaches wrestle with the thought, "Should I be more concerned with the team's performance on the floor or more concerned with making each player better?" We are convinced that by making each player better, the performance of the team will improve. That doesn't mean you forgo all team drills to work on individual skills, but it does mean devoting some time to also coaching players individually during practice. Shooting is an example of one skill that should be emphasized every day and should not be overlooked, but so are passing and dribbling.

Players place limitations on themselves and so do their parents, friends, fans and the media. As a coach, you should not place limitations on what your players can achieve. Players' abilities can always be improved if they are willing to expend the effort and will work hard at improving each day. Coaches should devote daily practice time to fundamentals and strive to improve every player in different phases of the game. If a big man isn't comfortable bringing the ball up the court, it's probably because he's never been given the opportunity to do so, even in practice. He probably has been told to give it to a guard and get out of the way. If you set up a drill that forces him to bring the ball up under pressure, then he'll become more proficient. Sometime during the season he may be put into a situation where he'll be forced to bring the ball up court. He'll no longer be limited to what other "big men" can't do. The same principle holds true when inbounding the ball on the baseline or sideline. Many players have never been exposed to inbounding the ball under pressure and, consequently, become error prone when forced to do so. Devote practice time to enable different players the opportunity to inbound the basketball. This also will help you decide which players are most capable of inbounding the ball under pressure.

If you are a beginning coach, choosing your style may initially come down to trial and error. Remember: Always try to expose your players to everything that can possibly happen in a basketball game. Prepare them for every eventuality. You can't ask your team to break a press unless it knows how to press. At the same time you teach your team how to press, you also should be teaching it how to break pressure. Make your drills competitive and strive for a successful conclusion of each and every play or possession. Practice should be realistic and should be devoted to adjusting to game situations. You might even want to practice against six or seven defensive players when attacking the press. This definitely will help your players concentrate and successfully deal with pressure.

Basketball is a game of mistakes. The team making fewer mistakes usually wins.

We often hear coaches say, "I spend 95 percent of my practice time working on defense." Well, in our opinion, they should be teaching offense at the same time. This is where you have an opportunity to utilize your assistant coach or coaches in your teaching. There's a lesson to be learned for everyone in every practice drill. It does not matter whether the player is on offense or defense in a given drill. Think about how football teams operate. In addition to the head coach, they have an offensive coordinator, a quarterback coach, a coach for the running backs, a receivers coach and/or a tight ends coach as well as a line coach. Then they have similar coaching positions for the defense and a special teams coach. In football they coach everyone at their respective positions, regardless of whether the emphasis in any drill is on offense or defense. Basketball coaches should do the same with all of their practice drills by fully involving their assistants in the teaching and planning process. This also helps emphasize to your players that your assistants have your respect and confidence. If there are only two of you, a good idea would be to have one coach handle the offense and one the defense.

Many coaches try to force-feed their systems to their teams year after year. Even if the system has been successful, you still must find out each year what the players feel comfortable doing, what they can do and what level of confidence they have in the team's style and philosophy. You only get that answer by communicating with your staff and players. Don't be afraid to ask what they think and try to ask questions that require more than a yes or no answer. Communicate. Encourage your players to express themselves. Get them to realize that you are dealing with them as people and not as X's and O's on a blackboard or a computer screen. They must understand not only that your job is to win, but that you also recognize you have a responsibility to help them become better basketball players. Find out what each player considers his or her strengths and weaknesses. If your tallest player tells you he isn't comfortable playing with his back to the basket, then work with him to get him more comfortable in that position. You might want to create situations enabling him to face the basket, thus helping him maximize his abilities.

We try to design and use drills to get this point across to our players. Coaches have to adjust to their personnel or they had better make certain they only have players that can plug into their system year after year. You have to recognize and accept the abilities of your players. Don't waste time dwelling on their deficiencies. If one player is better than the others at shooting off the dribble, then try to maximize those skills. If another player is a great offensive rebounder, make sure he is in position to go to the offensive board as often as possible, regardless of his size.

A team's most obvious leader is the head coach, but he must recognize, nurture and develop leadership qualities in his players. Not every player is a born leader. However, all teams will look to one or more players for positive guidance. Coaches must provide an environment that allows a team's leaders to step forward, assert themselves and assume this role. Coaches should respect the team's natural leaders and maintain an open dialogue with those players.

Players at all levels are alike. Whether you talk with an NBA all-star or a high school backup, every player wants to know his or her role. Anytime a player is unhappy or uncomfortable with his playing time, his response is, "Well, I don't understand my role." You can define that role only by communicating with the player. This requires more than one meeting at the beginning of the season and another at the end of the year. It necessitates constant communication on almost a daily basis. Communication is a two-way street. Just lecturing to the team will never completely get your point across and communicating with the team isn't necessarily a sign of weakness on the coach's part. It doesn't mean you are letting them question your authority. You're simply treating them like human beings. If you are interested in your players and communicate with them, you'll definitely get better results because they'll try harder to please you. This is hard work and coaches must realize that though all players have to be treated equally, there are many ways to skin a cat and the coach's job is to find out what motivates each player. You can listen and hear what they are saying and then it is your job to do what you feel should be done. Don't belittle your players or their games.

4

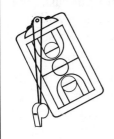

The five best players don't necessarily always start or play, but the five players who play the best together do.

Whatever the level, coaches should teach responsibility and discipline while they coach. Some coaches aren't concerned about what the players do off the court, but nevertheless, the players' actions usually are reflected on the court. If you can get your players to be responsible and consistent off the court, it'll carry over to the basketball floor. That's one way to win championships. Work with your players as people, not just as players. A great coach is a great communicator. He gets to be a great coach by talking with other coaches, going to clinics, by reading, by reviewing what he's done, by observing what other coaches do in various situations and by talking with his assistant coaches and players. He should never be satisfied and should keep up with the changing nature of the game. He must constantly review and constructively evaluate his coaching. He must also be willing to put in the time necessary for achieving success. Most importantly, the coach must be himself. Don't try to imitate someone's personality or style. If it isn't comfortable, don't do it. Good listeners usually make successful coaches.

Finally, figure out what you are comfortable teaching, recognize what your personnel is capable of doing and then challenge both yourself and your players to exceed expectations. Above all, communicate, exude confidence and demonstrate your interest in your players as people.

The keys to victory

- Basketball is a game of mistakes. The team that makes fewer mistakes normally wins. Stress to your players that you don't want them to make the same mistake twice. You should correct or point out every error, but sometimes in practice you must permit the players to run up and down the court without blowing the whistle every time a player doesn't do something correctly. You should let them play, establish a rhythm and permit them to learn to overcome errors to help them cope with adversity and to changing game situations.

- Practice doesn't make perfect; perfect practice makes perfect. We believe in perfect or correct repetition. It's not repetition just for the sake of making your players practice, but repetition so that everyone understands what it is you are trying to accomplish. Players need to be able to react instinctively to any situation on the court. That reaction comes from being exposed to the situation in practice and repeatedly working on it until recognition, response and reaction are automatic. You can best accomplish this

5

by working on the same drills daily with different looks and emphasis. For instance, it isn't punishment if you require players in shooting practice to successfully follow and rebound their misses. They learn to rebound offensively and also take more shots in almost the same period of time.

■ If you lose a close game and have 17 turnovers, get outrebounded by six rebounds on the offensive end and shoot just 67 percent from the free-throw line, you might want to point out that if each player had eliminated just one or two of his mistakes, you probably would have won the game. Everybody makes mistakes, but have your players work at eliminating as many as possible and not repeating the same errors. You have to talk about those mistakes in as positive a way as possible, but don't dwell on them. Compliment your players when they correct their mistakes. Motivate them to excel and recognize their improvement and achievements.

■ Many coaches believe that another key to winning is the belief that if an opponent is really good at something, you should try to mirror what they do and attack in the same manner. If they like to press, then press them right back. If they like to slow it down, then possibly make them play defense for a longer period of time by really executing your offense. Expose their weaknesses and capitalize on their deficiencies. Find their Achilles heal and exploit it by going for the jugular.

■ As a coach, you must exude confidence, and you have to make your players confident. Your players must go out on the court with the knowledge that you have prepared them to handle any situation that might arise and that you will adjust to changing situations during the game.

■ If you were given the choice of the kind of players you can have, what type would you select? We prefer aggressive, athletic players; players who will act, not always react; players capable of adjusting to any situation. Since coaches don't always get to select the players they want, sometimes their philosophy has to change according to the personnel they have. Be flexible and recognize what your talent can and cannot do and don't dwell on what you don't have. Maximize their strengths and minimize their weaknesses.

■ You must set goals, both short-term and long-term. In professional basketball, we always have the long-term goal of winning the NBA championship, but we also might establish a definite five-game goal, or a goal of where we want to be at the end of the month or by the All-Star Break. Another short-term goal would be what we want to accomplish on a particular road trip or home stand. We try to focus on goals that are realistic and achievable. You might want to make a goal as broad and general as: *We want to be better than we were last year at a certain time during the season*; or as specific as: *We need our guards to combine to get 10 rebounds a night.* Explain how many rebounds they can easily get off missed free throws or long rebounds near the free-throw line on a missed field-goal attempt if they really concentrate. To communicate those goals, put them in writing or post them on the blackboard or on a wall in the dressing room. You might even pass them out at a team meeting. Establish both team and individual goals; how many games you want to win at home and how many on the road.

■ You might want to meet before a game with the big players in one group and the small players in another and then encourage each group to meet separately. Discuss the opposing players and how to play them and how to help each other. Sit down with your big people and come up with realistic goals. Inform them as a group that you expect them, as a group, to get at least 10 offensive rebounds every game. Later, you might sit down with a particular individual and tell him that you are expecting him to grab five offensive rebounds each game. Be realistic with individual goals, but don't limit a player's individual ability. This is where you can define a player's role on the team. If the role you have in mind for a player is to come off the bench for 10 minutes a night and play good defense, then don't give him a goal of scoring 10 points a game. You'll confuse the player. A more realistic goal would be: *Hold the player you are guarding scoreless and have your team outscore the opposition while you are on the floor.*

Make the shot or get the **STOP**.

■ How do you handle not achieving your goals? Try to analyze why they weren't accomplished. Come up with a plan of how to achieve them the next time you play. Were the goals realistic? If not, why weren't they? Had you prepared your players adequately to achieve these goals? Try to communicate your conclusions and have your players verbalize their expectations and motivate them to over achieve.

■ You must stress fundamentals. Leave no stone unturned and prepare for any eventuality. Stress organization. Your players should know the role of every player on the floor. If you are teaching players to break a press, each player should know what every player on your team is supposed to do and why. You never know when a player might be forced to "play out of position." You also should teach — for the benefit of putting in your press defense as well — what each player on defense is trying to accomplish. For example, if your guards know that a certain type of press is designed to trap them in the corner or force them sideline, then they will know how to avoid bringing the ball to the corner and how to keep the ball in the middle of the floor. Each player should be aware of and know what each of the other nine players is supposed to be doing in any given situation.

■ Don't take anything for granted. Coaches don't like surprises. Try to anticipate and prepare for every possible situation. Your players must always be

 Players must be intense on defense, but on offense they should be relaxed and concentrate on trying to score or help their teammates score.

aware of the time, the score and the tempo of the game. Don't just send them out there and say, "We're going to run the box offense." They must know why you are using it, when you want to run it and what plays and options they are to call. A lot of coaches have offenses that they only use against man-to-man defenses. There's nothing wrong with that, but to be successful you need to run offenses and options that your players are confident will work against may different defenses.

■ Communicate. Don't assume that you know and see everything. Ask your assistant coaches, ask your players. They might spot something you overlooked or have taken for granted which might help you win a game. Have your point guard pick up the other team's signals and relay them to the bench and the other players on the floor during the game.

■ Start at the beginning every season. Walk the players through everything, from what they do the first day they come to practice (which locker they use, whether or not you want everyone's ankles taped, how they put on their socks to avoid getting blisters, what time to arrive for practice and games). No detail should be too small. You won't have to spend a week of practice going over all of this (unless you are coaching a grade school team), but don't assume that everyone knows everything. Rehearse your game night activities. Let your players know what time they should be in the locker room, how they should be dressed, where they should park their car or get dropped off, where their uniform will be, and whether the team will go on the court together or if they can go out on their own to shoot around if there is no preliminary game. Organize and explain what kinds of drills you'll run in the warm-ups, what stretching exercises should be done and when you do them, how the team lines up for the national anthem, where everyone sits on the bench, what you do during a timeout, what you do at halftime both in the locker room and when you come back onto the court, how you report into the game, what you do if you need medical attention during the game, what you do if you win the game and what you do should you lose, and what you do in the locker room after the game and how you want them to handle the media. All these procedures are important if you want good organization.

■ You might want to include all of this information in a Players' Handbook. Go over the contents of the handbook with your players. Don't assume that your players will read or understand everything in the handbook. What else should you include in your handbook? Perhaps all of your offensive and defensive sets, pertinent telephone numbers and addresses, a schedule, and team rules and regulations. Everyone wants to be disciplined, but not chastised for something that was overlooked but the coach took for granted because he assumed the players knew it was their responsibility. Review the rules and go over any changes that will be in effect each season.

■ The head coach should meet regularly with the point guards as a group to discuss responsibilities, just as a football coach meets with the quarterbacks. You might want an assistant coach to meet with other players, such as the big men or wings to discuss group and individual responsibilities. Do this on a regular basis, perhaps the day before a game, either before or after practice. Discuss the opponent's strengths and weaknesses and how you want to play them.

■ If you want to ensure victory, you should have the best conditioned team you can possibly have. Many coaches end practice with drills that stress concentration and running. We believe this is very important. Run drills that simulate game conditions, that emphasize concentration and demand successful execution. Make these drills five or six minutes in duration. They breed reacting and concentrating when the players are tired and the game might be on the line. If there are errors in execution, have the group go again. Force the players to recognize the importance of positive reaction and concentration when they are fatigued. Shoot free throws while the players are tired. Establish a number they have to make or have a goal each day; don't end practice until you've successfully reached your goal.

Little things win ballgames and championships. Be prepared. Don't overlook anything that can help you win a game.

More Keys to Victory

1. Outrebound opponents.

2. Don't give your opponents second shots.

3. Stop transition and easy baskets.

4. Limit your turnovers.

5. Take away what your opponent does best. Force them into options.

6. Penetrate. Get to the goal and cause the defense to make decisions.

7. Make the quick transition from offense to defense with all five players.

8. Keep their offense in front of you. Don't let anyone get behind you.

9. Run for layups and get easy baskets.

10. Make a high percentage of your free-throw attempts.

11. Be in great physical condition.

12. Above all, it is important to take advantage of the rules and make them work for you. In the NBA, zones are not permitted and therefore many teams try to bend the rules and run isolations (one-on-one plays) and plays designed for two or three players to spread the court and take away defensive help.

Coaches should use the shot clock and game clock in practice.

 # Communication

Working with your Players

Treat every day as a new day. Don't ever carry grudges. If you had a bad day or you or a player blew up the day before, you be the one to defuse any carryover the next day. When you see the player come into practice you might want to acknowledge him to have him realize you won't be holding anything against him and that today is indeed a new day.

Remember that every player is part of the team, regardless if that player is the best player or the 12th man. Try to speak to every player every day. Speak to players individually if you sense there is a problem or they don't appear to understand their roles.

I can't play everybody, but I can and must coach every one of my players.

Respect your players as people at all times. Let them know that positive and constructive dissent is acceptable. You must be willing to discuss anything. Don't become a dictator who is unapproachable. You might also want to exhibit an

Communicate with your players and respect them as people at all times. Let them know that you're approachable and willing to discuss anything. (Photo©Frank McGrath)

interest in their affairs away from basketball. You as a coach probably spend more time with your players than anyone other than their parents or families. They probably look to you for guidance in critical or difficult situations. Don't be afraid to discipline them if it is necessary. They'll understand and respect your discipline as long as it is consistent and fair. Players expect to be disciplined.

Utilizing Your Staff

Every head coach should have a staff that complements him. If the head coach is a defensive-minded coach, then at least one of the assistants should have a strong understanding of offensive basketball. If the head coach is a screamer at practice, then find an assistant who can diffuse difficult situations when they need to be diffused.

You must communicate with your staff. Encourage them to speak up. Ask them questions that require more than a yes or no answer. Encourage them to speak with the players. Encourage them to teach, but let them know what you want emphasized. You must treat every assistant with respect, both in front of the team and in closed door meetings. If you don't respect your staff, you might as well not have one. Treat them fairly and equally. If you want loyalty you must demonstrate that it is a two-way street.

Recognize the contributions of your staff both privately and publicly.

Give them specific responsibilities in practice and administratively. Also be aware that most assistant coaches would like to be head coaches some day. Give them experience to become a head coach and help place them in a head coaching position if the opportunity arises. Show an interest in their careers. Don't be the kind of head coach who surrounds himself with assistants who don't have ambition or assistants who he knows are not prime head coaching material.

During the game, give the assistants specific roles. Have one responsible for offense and another for defense. Perhaps one takes inside players and another takes perimeter players. Develop a chart that the assistants can keep that will help you analyze what is happening, but don't make busy work for them. Utilize their information. Have them realize that it is important to your team's success. Make sure what you have them chart is something you can use during the game or at halftime. Perhaps you can have someone chart which plays both teams are running, their success rate and the number and success rate of fast breaks or second-chance opportunities.

Establish a rule that prohibits a coach from publicly correcting another coach who is working individually with a player. Do not permit anyone to contradict a coach when he is working with a player. It is very important that players realize how much confidence and respect the coaching staff has for each other's abilities.

Making a
Checklist

Prepare an annual checklist of key points of emphasis you as a coach feel you need to cover. Each of these points should be introduced, explained and reviewed during the preseason, in-season and again when preparing for postseason competition. Make sure that you review and revise this list prior to your next season.

A. Jump ball theory

    1. Offensive setup

    2. Defensive setup

    3. Where to channel the tap if you can't control the tip

B. The last shot in the quarter or half (LSQ or LSH) — clock management

    1. Offensive sets (configuration if different from normal offensive alignment)

        a. When to look for the shot (time on the shot clock)

        b. Who do you want to shoot? First and second options

        c. Rebounding and defensive balance responsibilities

    2. How to defense various sets

        a. Type of defense

        b. When and how to pressure

C. The last shot in the game (LSG) — clock management

    1. Offensively

        a. When to take it

        b. The first and second options

        c. Anticipate the miss

        d. Opportunity to rebound

    2. Defensively

        a. Deny and double-team the ball; get it out of the primary scorer's hands

        b. Set up a possible steal situation

        c. Invert and switch all crosses

        d. Pressure the ball

        e. Box out and get the rebound

Players are always responsible for knowing the time, score and how many timeouts each team has remaining, and if possible, the personal foul and bonus situation.

Emphasize that whether you are on offense or defense, you must not stand around and pray the ball will go in or will miss. Anticipate the miss and rebound. Take nothing for granted. Recover the ball or put it back in the basket.

D. How to line up on the free-throw line

    1. Offensively

        a. Box out

        b. Know the shooter's percentage

        c. Discuss particular strategies

        d. Practice how to purposely miss if you need to score more than one point with little or almost no time left

    2. Defensively

        a. Who takes the shooter?

        b. Boxing out. Where to play strongest rebounder

        c. Pinching

        d. Crashing

E. Full-court pressure defense

    1. Man-to-man or zone

    2. How to build a press

        a. Pressure the inbounds passer

        b. No pressure on the inbounds passer

        c. Trapping on the first pass before the dribble

        d. Trapping on the first dribble

        e. Doubling the ball from behind

        f. Doubling the ball from in front

        g. Configuration and responsibilities of players not involved in the trap

        h. Level back to the ball on passes over your head

        i. Release quickly and get out of the trap once the pass is made

        j. Signals to be used to identify the defense you want to play

F. Half-court pressure defense

    1. Man-to-man or zone

        a. Where to pick up, channel and pressure the ball

        b. Where to force the ball

        c. Doubling from behind

        d. Doubling from in front

        e. Configuration and responsibilities of players not involved in pressuring or actually trapping the ball

        f. Fronting the low post

        g. Doubling or trapping the low post

G. Fast break off a free throw

    1. Organization (various sets)

    2. Responsibilities of individual players

    3. Positioning your players

H. Transition defense

    1. See the ball at all times

    2. Responsibility of all five players to get level with or in front of the ball

    3. Build defense from the basket out, 94 feet

    4. Stop and pressure the ball. Make them pick it up

    5. Do you pressure the rebounder?

    6. Do you deny the outlet?

    7. Tandem defense

    8. Talk. Pick up the free men nearest the basket

        a. Don't go back to your defensive assignment if someone else picked him up in transition; Get his or the most dangerous free man

I. Transition offense

    1. 94 feet. Then in, out and over. Make the defense cover

    2. Do you inbound to one man in particular?

    3. Decide which man takes it out after a field goal. How quickly do you want to inbound the ball?

    4. Who inbounds after a free throw?

    5. Decide if wings should pop to the corners or cross on the break if they can't get a layup

J. Signals when a play breaks down

    1. Do you want a particular player to have the ball?

    2. What play do you want to run?

    3. When do you want to penetrate (time left on the shot clock)?

K. Side out of bounds (SOB)

    1. Offensively

        a. Purpose: Inbound ball safely first; look to score second

        b. Score immediately off a set play

        c. First, second and third options

    2. Defensively

        a. Where to channel the ball; how to pressure

        b. How to defend the player inbounding the ball

        c. The inbounds passer is always an offensive threat

        d. Special defenses for special situations

            1. Man-to-man or zone

            2. Time on shot and game clock

            3. Areas of the court

L. Baseline out of bounds (BOB)

    1. Offensively; first, second and third options

    2. Defensively

        a. Man-to-man or zone

        b. Where to channel the ball

        c. How to guard the player inbounding the ball

You should practice taking the ball out of bounds from the corners, end line, etc., and also definitely practice your out-of-bounds plays with varying amounts of time on the game and shot clocks. Think also how many inbounding opportunities teams have during a game.

M. Fast-break organization

    1. Sideline break

    2. Middle break

    3. Long passes and/or outlets

    4. Dribble break

    5. Break after makes

    6. Break after misses

    7. On foul shots

    8. Out of bounds in backcourt

N. Four-minute drill

    1. How often do you want to drill on this phase of the game?

    2. Score and time (clock management)

    3. Special situations

        a. Free throw

        b. Side out

        c. When and what play will you run when you need to score?

O. Two-minute drill (with your team losing), or with less time on the clock

    1. Score and time (clock management)

    2. When, if and whom to foul

    3. When not to foul

Use verbal or hand signs to inform players of which strategy to use: To foul or lock in and play for a stop. You must eliminate confusion and incorrect communication.

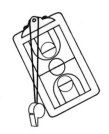

Each turnover gives you one less possession and one less opportunity to score. It also gives your opponent an additional scoring opportunity.

P. Defending a great scorer: special strategy

Q. Video
    1. Locker room
    2. Before or after walk-through at day of game shoot-around
    3. Day after games
    4. Collectively as a team
    5. Individual player conferences

R. Bench conduct
    1. No technical fouls
    2. Support system — encouragement and enthusiasm

S. Utilizing timeouts
    1. When to call them
        a. Too early, a sign of weakness
        b. Gives your opponent additional preparation time
    2. Special need situations
    3. Save for unexpected developments

T. Recognizing and taking advantage of foul situations
    1. 1-and-1 opportunities
    2. Players in jeopardy

U. Substitutions and matchups
    1. Defensive changes
    2. Height or skill advantage
    3. End of game or period; offense/defense

V. Full-court press offense
    1. Do you want to score or simply advance the ball to the frontcourt to set up your half-court offense?
    2. Rules
    3. Responsibilities
    4. Method of attack

W. Half-court trap offense
    1. Do you want to score or simply advance the ball to the frontcourt to set up your half-court offense?
    2. Rules
    3. Responsibilities
    4. Method of attack

X. Passing the ball
    1. Forgotten or neglected art
    2. Under pressure
    3. Drills

Y. Scouting reports
    1. Who scouts?
    2. How to best utilize the reports
    3. When and how to present them to the team
    4. Drills in practice
    5. Do you scout your team?
        a. Who scouts your team?
        b. When (time of season)?
        c. How often?

Teaching Your System and Philosophy

We believe you best build rapport and understanding through positive reinforcement. Some coaches don't want to get too close to players, preferring to remain at a distance, because they think the players will take advantage of them. They look upon getting too involved with players as a sign of weakness. Do what you as a coach are most comfortable with. Stand up and accept responsibility and blame if doing so doesn't make you uncomfortable. If you make a mistake, admit it to the players. Your players should understand that you are always going to be honest with them and that you hold yourself to as high a standard as you hold them. **STRONG MEN CRITICIZE THEMSELVES**.

Remember, in our opinion you cannot fool them. Don't ever compromise your values, principles or beliefs, however. Don't take credit for the wins and put the blame for losses on somebody else. That's the easiest way to lose respect. Winning and losing are team efforts and are the responsibility of everyone connected with the team. If your players play hard and try to execute what you're asking them to do, then you must encourage them. Make them realize, "If we work hard every day in practice and bust our butts, and if we work harder than anybody else, we're definitely going to win. We're going to overachieve or maximize our abilities." Have them understand that it is not your job to coach effort. That is their individual responsibility.

It's a good idea every day before practice to announce and discuss what you are going to emphasize that session. "Today we're going to concentrate on offensive rebounding," "Today we're going to concentrate on getting back on defense and not giving transition baskets," or "Today we must make sure the fifth man in the break realizes he must trail the play because he is responsible for defensive balance and defending a quick transition."

You need to decide how much time you are going to devote to going half-court or full-court in your practice drills. You have to decide if you want the ball going inside first and then out, or outside and then inside. Do you want your offense beginning with your post players or ending with them. Develop drills that are competitive, simulate and re-create game situations. Instill and insist on learning how to win in all of your practices and drills. Balanced and consistent effort should be your goal. Make your players execute and play hard.

Coaches can't teach effort, but they can emphasize its importance. If your team goes out and plays as hard as it can and loses because the other team is better, that's acceptable, as long as everyone gave a complete effort. To improve effort, you have to make your team realize that it is expected to play and practice hard all the time and that hustle plays can make the difference between winning and losing. You have to give credit to your team for playing hard. Conversely, you must also let them know when you are not pleased and when they are not playing hard. It may sound simplistic, but sometimes players don't realize what effort is. You need to explain it to them. You must design drills that force players to work hard. Get them into the mind-set of working hard all the time. Set up competitive situations and make them successfully complete each drill. Get them used to winning and savoring success.

When correcting a player's mistake, it is sometimes better to first compliment him on something he's done well to get his attention. Then you can point out and correct his error. Encourage him to understand that you are trying to make him a better player and are not criticizing him personally. Correct mistakes as soon as possible instead of accepting them. Don't wait until the next day's practice to point them out unless you are addressing the team as a whole.

Let your players make mistakes and then correct them in a positive manner to help them improve.

 # Practice

Philosophy

Be conscious of keeping practice interesting. Try to vary and change your drills and the order of your drills every so often to combat losing your team's interest and concentration. Make drills competitive. You need to instill the will to win. If you have a shooting drill, keep score and reward the winners. Make the players want to win and have them relish the feeling of accomplishment as a reward for a job well done.

We prefer everything we do in practice to include using a basketball. Some coaches like to run suicide sprints and work on agility or whatever. That's not wrong, but we believe that you should incorporate the ball in everything you ask your players to do. This helps develop eye-hand coordination with players constantly moving in the basketball environment. In addition, it makes sense that any drill that requires a shot should be completed successfully. Whether it's a warm-up weave or 5-on-0 fast-break drill, every sequence must end with the ball going through the basket and should be run correctly. Have players inbound the ball after a score. Don't permit the players to cut corners. It's said that whenever Jerry Rice, the great wide receiver for the San Francisco 49ers, catches a pass in practice, he turns and runs to the goal line. That's what he wants to accomplish in a game, so that's the way he practices — all out, 100 percent every play. It's the same on the basketball court. If you want to score every trip down the court, then score every time in every drill, even if it takes three shots against a phantom defense. Your best players should set the example, just like Jerry Rice, Michael Jordan, Magic Johnson, Reggie Miller or Larry Bird. Make the most of every single possession.

You must also try to recognize when and if players are tired and you should give them a day off or run a shorter, more relaxed or different kind of practice.

Develop drills that are not only competitive, but also relate to game situations. Again, try to have every drill include a basketball. Drills should not be punishment. There should be a purpose to every drill. You may occasionally want to run a drill just to lighten things up, but every drill should prepare your players for a situation that might come up in a game.

Perfection is the result of execution and repetition.

Players must understand that they are expected to come to practice every day, and they are expected to come to practice on time every day prepared to give an honest effort. This is their charge. They have a responsibility to themselves, their teammates and the organization or school they represent. Explain to your players what you expect of them. Recognize when they are doing well by complimenting them. They want to know when they are performing well and should realize when they are not playing well or are letting the team down. Players are creatures of habit and generally remember only the bad things you say to them. Make a point of recognizing their accomplishments and positive performances before you point out their mistakes. Keep your players off guard and on their toes so they don't get complacent. There is always room for improvement, and you should challenge your players to want to get better.

Your players should always stretch before beginning all-out practice and again at the completion of practice. Regardless of whether you have a strength coach, trainer or player lead the stretching, everyone should stretch. This also provides a good time for a coach to go around and talk to players individually or to talk to the entire team about your plans for that day's practice and how the team can build on what was accomplished during the previous day's practice or game. Get your players immediately focused on what is expected that day. Coaches might even want to stretch with their players to help emphasize the importance of proper warm-ups and total team commitment.

We like to use the full court in our drills as much as we can. It definitely helps with conditioning, but it also makes players realize that the game is a 94-foot game on both offense and defense. We try to make practice realistic and as much like a game as possible. If the ball goes through the basket, we want the player nearest the ball or the designated inbounder to quickly take the ball out of bounds before the defense establishes itself, then push it up to the other end of the floor.

A Sample Practice Plan

A written plan should be developed in a coaches' meeting following a practice or prior to the next practice. Naturally, the level of play and the time available, dictates when you decide to meet.

Date: 11/30   Time: 10:30 a.m.   Place: Market Square Arena

Time .... Drill Emphasis

10:30-10:45 .... Group stretching

10:45-11:08 .... Fast-break organization
a. 3-man lane warm-up
b. 3-man crossing
c. 4-man crossing
d. 5-man transition into early offense
e. 5-man transition into set offense
f. SOB and BOB
g. Fast break off FT (press offense)
h. Fast break off FT (EOQ and EOG)
i. Shot clock situations

11:10-11:15 .... Shooting, full court jump shots (groups of three)

11:15-11:20 .... Defensive stations
a. 1-on-1   b. wing overplay

11:20-11:24 .... Defensive stations
a. 2-on-2   b. pick-and-roll   c. wing and middle

11:24-11:32 .... Shell defense
a. 4-on-4   b. half-court options

11:32-11:40 .... Fast break
a. 3-on-2   b. 2-on-1   c. 4-on-3   d. 3-on-1

11:46-11:52 .... Water break and shooting drill, big and small, both baskets, 3 men, 2 balls, all options

11:52-12:00 .... 4-on-4, 5-on-5, full court, press offense and defense, up and back

12:00-12:03 .... 5-on-5, full court, press offense following a free throw, i.e., press defense

12:03-12:07 .... 3-on-3, half-court "stops," all options

12:07-12:11 .... 4-on-4, half-court "stops," all options

12:11-12:17 .... 5-on-5, full-court transition, EOQ situations

12:17-12:26 .... 5-on-5, SOB and BOB plays, makers-takers with transition if miss

12:26-12:33 .... Water break, shooting, 2 stations, big and small, post moves, 2-man situations

12:33-12:43 .... Scrimmage, game and shot clock, shoot free throws

12:43-12:48 .... 2-minute drill, 5-on-5, setup situations, up 5, down 5, etc.

12:48-12:52 .... Free throws, 2 groups, 2 baskets, each group must make seven in a row before stopping

12:52-1:02 .... Group stretching

1:02- .... Individual work

The length of practice depends on rules, time of season, a day before a game, etc. There is no hard and fast rule as to the length of a practice.

Sample Practice Card for Coaches

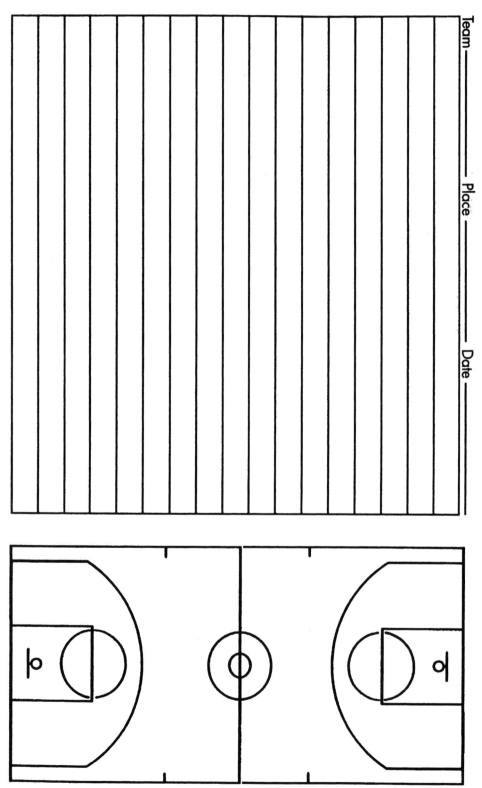

Sample Practice Card for Coaches

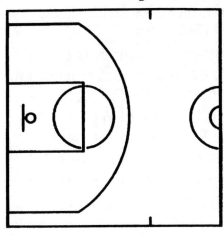
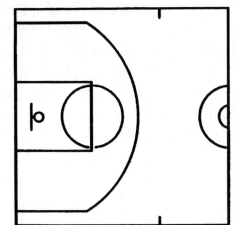

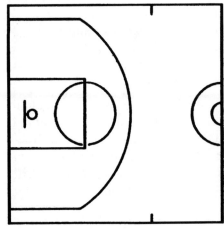
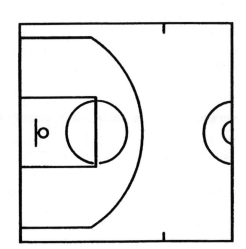

Example of a Defensive Practice Drill
4-on-3 and 5-on-4 Half-Court

The offense has the man advantage, but can only score on a layup. Jump shots must be contested and closed out, however, by defenders pressuring the ball. The defense must get a **stop** before changing to offense. We can also go full-court 4-on-3 or 5-on-4, but then we come back 3-on-3 with the shooter or turnover man out of the mix.

If we are letting players scrimmage, unless there is a glaring mistake, we let the scrimmage progress before pointing out an error. Players hate to scrimmage and have it stopped every trip down the floor. We don't ignore a major error, though, and we use natural stops in the play to make quick points. If you feel it necessary, substitute a player on the fly to review a mistake on the sideline without disrupting the flow of the scrimmage. Maybe you can scrimmage in short bursts, say six baskets, keeping time and score, and then review some of the more glaring mistakes while they take a short break. Sometimes it isn't a bad idea to let the winning team stay on the floor, only changing the five players that lost the scrimmage. Reward success! Always use the shot and game clocks whenever possible. You can use stops in practice to work on special situations and out-of-bounds plays. Both areas are easily overlooked and neglected during practice.

 Run every drill with a ball and stress successful completion.

Utilize some variety in the drills you use in your practices. It becomes monotonous and drudgery if you only work on four or five things in a practice, and you should try to keep each of your drills short. Use stations manned by assistants to cover additional points you need to address by breaking down into either big- and small-man groups or mixing up your players to cover game situations such as the pick-and-roll, emphasizing both offense and defense.

A lot of coaches believe that basketball games are a series of two- and three-man situations; if that's what you believe, then have a lot of drills and scrimmages that feature two-on-two, three-on-three and four-on-four, in addition to five-on-five competition. Practice these drills on the full and half court because that is the way the game is played. Many coaches alternate offensive and defensive drills to keep practice interesting and competitive. A coach's responsibility is to teach. We should never forget that.

In the NBA, many shots occur after only one or two passes. At other levels, you might want the team to make four or five passes before a shot is taken. That's something you need to emphasize in your drills. Have your players run their plays all the way through to teach the importance of changing sides with the ball and learning all of a particular play's options.

Use shooting drills to also work on rebounding. Chart where misses usually bounce from shots taken from different parts of the court. Make your team aware that longer shots produce longer rebounds and that shots from one corner more often than not can produce rebounds to the opposite corner. Repetition makes rebounding become a natural reaction. Great rebounders anticipate the miss and really go after the basketball. They always follow the flight of the ball as it leaves the shooter's hand to help them be in the right spot when the ball caroms off the rim or backboard.

Bad shots are like turnovers. They start opponents' fast breaks and limit your scoring opportunities.

Again, use stations to teach. Break the squad into small groups and make use of the whole court and all baskets. Have your assistant coaches assist you. You'll have fewer players standing around, and you'll get much more accomplished.

Break your drills into five- or seven-minute intervals. You can use the game clock to time various drills and to rotate your groups.

When you shoot in practice, create game situations and have players shoot from different spots on the floor. Make these drills meaningful and competitive. Utilize players as passers if the drill requires a person to pass. That helps to develop their overall game and passing ability.

Utilize your assistant coaches and staff as much as possible. We can always use another set of eyes and an extra voice. One coach can watch the big men, another the perimeter players. One coach can concentrate on the offense, another on the defense. Every player deserves to be watched and critiqued by a coach. Give every player feedback throughout the drills and scrimmages. Every man is an integral part of the team and is responsible for the team's progress and success.

Practice doesn't make perfect. Perfect practice makes perfect.

Methods of Teaching and Conducting Practices

We like to prepare daily and also weekly practice plans. As a staff we review these each day after practice and also at the end of every week. We try to estimate how much time we need to spend on certain situations and then evaluate our progress to see if the allotted time was sufficient or how much more time might be necessary in the coming weeks. For example, if you have a six-week preseason, you need to have a broad outline and know what you want to accomplish and cover each day and every week. You should have a checklist of what you want to accomplish by the first game and how you wish to augment this list during the rest of the season. Coaching and teaching occur during the entire season, not just in the preseason. Your job is never finished.

In the NBA, we have only 28 days to prepare for our first regular-season game, and during this period we also have to factor in time for eight exhibition games and travel days. We have to take into account injuries to key players or how tired our team might be. The coach is also responsible for his team's conditioning! Develop your practices so you have individual time and team time. Eliminate boredom, but not at the expense of neglecting areas necessary to make your team better and more competitive. You may also want to vary the length of your practices. If you always practice an hour and a half, players sense when a practice is nearly over and will either pace themselves or gear up for the end of it. You need to keep them off-balance. Have them realize that you'll work them as hard as it takes to get something done. If you have to work a little harder or longer on something, then the players should expect to go longer, realizing that it is for the team's benefit. Learn to utilize your time in the most efficient manner. Sometimes you need to give the players a day off if you sense they are physically or mentally spent.

Before planning your practice schedule, you should talk with your assistants. Find out what they think needs to be covered or emphasized. You should also develop a relationship with your captain. Call him in and ask him what the team feels it needs to work on. What is the team happy and comfortable running and what makes them uncomfortable, and why? You have to be in tune with the players' needs. You don't necessarily have to do what they want, but you should let them know you are sensitive to their opinions.

Decide when you prefer to teach new things. We sometimes introduce new things at the end of practice when the team is tired. Why? Because we feel forcing our players to concentrate when they are tired will carry over to games and will help us win. Your players must be able to concentrate at the end of a game, even if they are tired. That doesn't mean waiting until the team has practiced for three hours before you teach a new offense. But it means instead of introducing it early in the practice, wait until you've done 30-40 minutes of drills before teaching a new thing. Other coaches introduce new plays or concepts at the beginning of practice. Use whatever method makes you comfortable. Positive reaction to stress and tiredness helps win games and championships. Some coaches will have strenuous running drills with the ball to end practice because concentration is of the utmost importance when players are tired and must execute. Many games go down to the wire before they are won, and the best-conditioned team usually has the best chance of winning.

Explain what you are trying to teach and why. When introducing a new play or defense, you might want to introduce it to the players utilizing a blackboard, by demonstrating it on the basketball floor, at a team meeting or maybe even with a video to familiarize them with it. Walk the players through it and help them visualize it. Break it down into component parts and then work on it as a unit. Review it once more before beginning to scrimmage. Encourage questions and try to answer them as soon as they come up if they are pertinent. Always stress and demand the correct timing, proper floor spacing and defensive balance.

Emphasize fundamentals and be consistent in your approach. Demand correct execution through constant repetition and prepare your team for the options it will have to rely on if the first one doesn't work or if your opponent suddenly changes his offensive or defensive tactics.

5-on-5 Practice Drill
(To work on and also defend the passing game)

Once we have explained our rules we can work on this drill either by permitting or not permitting the players to dribble once the required five passes have been made before we attempt a shot. We might relax the five passes rule if an offensive player is free for an uncontested layup. We want to encourage our players to help one another at all times, both offensively and defensively.

Rules:

With the ball on the wing below the free-throw line, the strongside post man can: post up, step up and screen the ball on the wing, screen across the lane or step out to the corner as an outlet if the ball handler is in trouble.

The weakside players are instructed to interchange off the ball by downscreening or backpicking each other on our buddy system. They are to free each other and occupy the defense. We want to pass to the first free man. We want our big players to set screens on the ball and roll to the goal if they are not posting up. The weakside big man would then step up on the roll.

Our outside men are required, once they pass, to screen on the ball or make a hard basket cut. We want the players to work with their buddies by staying on the same side of the court because we can always change sides with the ball from the top on a guard-to-guard type of pass. If the wing cannot pass the ball on the side with only himself and a post man, the post man can step up the lane to help relieve the defensive pressure.

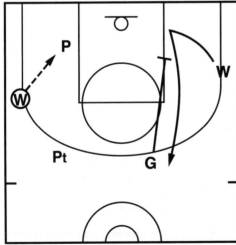

Strongside ball below the foul line. Post up when the wing has the ball.

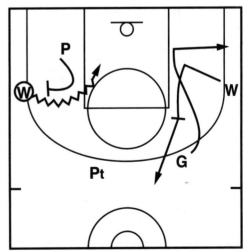

The post steps up and screens the wing.

5-on-5 Practice Drill
(To work on and also defend the passing game)

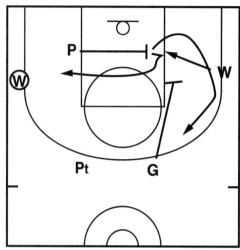

The post screens across.

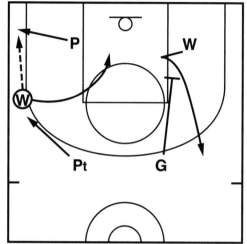

The post steps out as an outlet; the wing cuts to the goal.

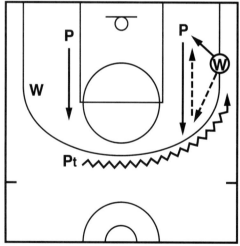

Side with two players: point and post, wing and post.

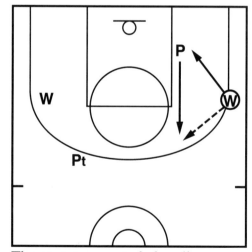

The post steps up to help relieve pressure; the wing passes and cuts.

5-on-5 Practice Drill
(To work on and also defend the passing game)

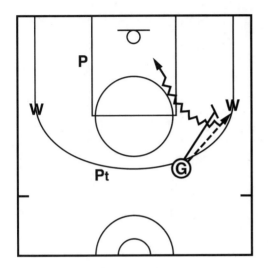

The outside men are passing and screening on the ball.

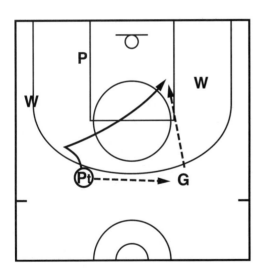

The outside man is passing and cutting to receive the pass.

Defensive

Principles

You should decide whether you want to teach pressure defense, perimeter defense, pressure man-to-man, zone defense, pressure zone or a combination of the above. Figure out if you want to be primarily a zone or man-to-man team and whether or not you want to play a half-court or full-court defense. Perhaps you favor playing multiple defenses. After deciding what you want to play, then decide how you want to teach defense. We believe you build defense through one-on-one, two-on-two, three-on-three and four-on-four drills based on strong man-to-man principles and fundamentals. Once your team is well-schooled in man-to-man fundamentals, you then can teach zone principles if you so desire because you have established a sound fundamental man-to-man defensive foundation.

Part of which defense you choose to play depends on your available personnel and how you can maximize the rules you play under. Most importantly, your decision should be based on what you feel gives you the best chance of winning night after night.

Some things to consider here are:

■ Do you want to play perimeter defense from the three-point line on out or the three-point line on in?

■ Do you want to force the ball toward the sideline and baseline or funnel it to the middle of the court?

■ Do you want to double-team, trap, and or run and jump?

- Do you want to switch when any players cross or only when equals cross?

- Where do you want the defense to actually pick up your opponents and begin to apply pressure?

- How do you want to play when the dribble is alive, and how do you want to play when the dribble is dead?

- How should you play the men on the weak side and how do you want to play the man on the strong side without the ball?

- Do you want to play in front, behind or three-quarter a man in the pivot without the ball?

- How do you want to play a man that goes backdoor when you overplay and deny him the ball?

Weakside defenders should know where the ball is. Strongside defenders should know where their man is.

How do you best determine what you want your team to do in each of these situations? Study and evaluate your personnel. If you have a big guy who can block shots, you might funnel the dribbler into his area. When a team likes to run a play to a certain side, you might decide to force it to the opposite sideline, away from its strength. Many of the philosophical and tactical decisions you make come from experience and/or trial and error, but you can also pick up a lot by going to clinics, and by observing and talking to other coaches. By studying your trade, you learn that certain principles might work better than others. Probably the most important basic defensive principle is to stop penetration. Your team must do whatever is necessary in order to stop the ball from penetrating closer to the basket. Strong defensive coaching principles emphasize not allowing an opponent's offense to change sides with the basketball. Accomplish this by teaching pressuring and overplaying the ball. You must practice this on a daily basis.

Most coaches emphasize pressuring the ball, keeping your man in front of you and contesting every pass and shot. If your opponent has picked up his dribble, get all over him. Make it difficult for him to pass to his outlets by pressuring the ball to help teammates who are denying the outlets.

Teaching defense begins by coaching your players in positioning, stance and how to guard the man with the ball. Then progress by teaching how you want to guard a man without the ball who is one pass away. Determine and teach how you want to defend a lateral pass as opposed to a penetrating pass. Defense is intensity, anticipation, concentration and desire, but it must be constantly practiced, emphasized and rewarded.

Devote time to teaching how to make the transition from guarding a man with the ball to guarding a man without the ball by teaching your players how to move and step in the direction of the pass, especially when the ball is in the air, not when it is caught. Do you drop to the level of the ball or deny him? The answer to that should be part of your overall defensive philosophy.

Teach your players how you want them to play a cutter. Do you want them to chuck, bump and ride, or deny? Set up drills and stations to practice each situation.

Do you want to contest every shot? Do you want a hand up every time a player shoots? Explain this tactic as a way to alter the shot so you lower the shooter's percentage. Have your players realize that basketball is a game of angles and percentages and taking advantage of those wins championships. Then take this a step further by teaching the importance of boxing out.

Set up drills where you practice playing one-on-one, then two-on-two, three-on-three and four-on-four from different areas of the court. Set up different situations and work on each of them. Remember, you also must work on defending when the offense has a man advantage as well as scoring from these different offensive situations.

The ball will continue to take you to your man if you lose him as long as you open up, keep your eye on the ball and continue to retreat to the goal.

Defensive Rules

Emphasize the ones you feel are most important to teach in your system.

1. Screening
   a. Squeezing the diagonal backpick from the weak side.
   b. Slip the pick on the downscreen on the weak side. Don't let them screen you. MOVE.
   c. Decide if you want to force and ride the baseline cutter high or low and whether the screener's defender should bump him.
   d. Don't chase the backpicker. Talk and help. You can bump and/or switch when your man sets a backpick.

2. Switching
   a. Switching is a fine tactic, but only after you first teach and establish strong and definite standard man-to-man defensive rules prohibiting switching. Once your basic man-to-man defensive fundamentals have been established, you can be flexible and prepared to make adjustments during games or when practicing to play and take advantage of a particular opponent's weaknesses.

b. We can decide to switch equal-sized players on crosses and screens automatically as well as diagonal or vertical up blocks or downscreens between equals, but only when each player understands and is aware of what we are doing. We can also decide to switch everything, regardless of size. Much depends on the opponent we are facing.

c. On a pindown from small to big, we can switch or invert to keep the big man home.

d. Decide if you switch dribble handoffs, trap them or slide through?

e. Practice against defending the curl, recurl and screen on the curl.

f. Talk and come together, and talk on switches. Don't let the offense split the defenders.

3. Transition

a. In transition, it is the responsibility of the first man back to cover the goal and contain or slow up the offense until help arrives. The second man back forms a tandem to help keep the offense from penetrating. Force them to throw an extra pass until help arrives. Your players should stay level with the ball and use their hands and arms to clog and pressure the passing lanes.

4. Basic Defensive Rules

a. Every defensive player should always see the ball.

b. Always try to get level with the ball if your offensive opponent trails the play. Help stop penetration.

c. Keep the dribbler in front of you and limit penetration.

d. Pressure the passer if his dribble is used up. Move your arms and hands. Get deflections. Force the pass where you want it to go. Pressure the pass and help men defending cutters.

e. Place yourself at the point of the "V" in the ball-you-man principle.

f. Have a defense set up to defend every type of isolation play.

g. Concentrate. Don't commit three-point shot fouls.

h. Don't give up layups. Make them shoot and make free throws.

i. Fake at dribblers to break their rhythm. Don't let a dribbler call a play comfortably. Pressure him, but contain his dribble penetration.

j. Deny and make wings catch the ball farther out to start their offense.

k. Yell empty, ice or your predetermined signal when guarding a cutter who empties out after his cut. Let the man guarding the ball know he is alone. Don't chase your man. Remain in the lane to help a teammate.

l. Explain to your teammate that he is alone. Let him know where to force the iced offensive player (inside toward the middle or to the baseline).

m. Use your hands and extend your arms to clog and impede the passing lanes. Try to deflect the pass, but don't foul.

n. Get five men in the paint to stop penetration.

o. Stay attached to the weakside post man to prevent him from making the lob pass.

p. Pressure the dribbler and make him change direction by getting to his outside hand and shoulder each time he changes direction. This may cause a turnover.

q. One of our goals is to prohibit our opponents from reversing the ball on offense.

r. Standardize and establish your defensive rules. You can adjust for specific opponents when the need arises.

s. Don't gamble for steals, scramble or commit foolish fouls with the shot clock running down. Lock in and play D.

t. Don't follow your man on a weakside downscreen away from the ball. Slide through.

u. On the strongside turnout, chase your man. Don't go over the top or slide through unless an adjustment has been discussed.

v. Develop the mentality to defend and box out for 24 seconds or for the full time of the shot clock, not just for 20 seconds. Defend every possession.

w. Overplay penetrating passes and force the offensive player backdoor. Be confident that your weakside defenders will cover your back. Force them to make a great play to beat you.

x. On backpicks off pindowns, force the player coming off the pindown to the outside or make him curl.

y. Decide if you want to open up and retreat if beaten backdoor or if you want to turn your back on the ball and face-guard your man to deny him the ball.

z. Double-team all baseline drives with the strongside post man or nearest defender.

aa. Front all postups.

bb. Three-quarter and bump post men off the low post.

cc. If playing behind the post, keep moving to disconcert your opponent.

5. Tactics

a. Switch and invert on the weak side. Keep the ball to one side of the court. Don't let them reverse the ball.

b. Switch up the line when defending multiple and staggered screens.

c. Don't permit the trapped player to get the ball back once he passes out of the trap or double-team. Step toward the ball as it is passed.

d. Call out and talk on all screens.

e. Change up your defenses, but contest every defensive possession.

f. Apply full-court pressure. Make your opponent use up the time needed to run half-court offenses.

g. Use the run-and-jump to make opposing point guards relinquish the ball. Don't commit and run until you are within six feet of the ball. Cause the pass to be thrown over your outside shoulder.

h. Deny the point guard the ball after a score. Get to him quickly. Make weaker ball handlers advance the ball under pressure.

i. Against bigger teams, you may want to extend the defense and pick the point man up higher. Pressure and contain him.

6. Shooters

a. Keep your hands up and contest each shot to cut down shooting percentages.

b. Make shooters dribblers and force them out of their range. Make them put the ball on the floor with their weak hand.

c. Crack the best shooter before he shoots. Don't let him get his rhythm. Break his flow and concentration.

d. Many NBA players block shots when two hands come to the ball. You might want to teach players how to do this as a sometimes tactic.

e. Try to block, impede or contest shots with the hand nearest the ball, not across your body.

f. Be alert. You can block shots off the ball from behind when a shooter turns his back to you.

g. Block shots from the weak side off the ball.

h. Perimeter defenders must see the ball when it is inside. If the shooter turns his back, the nearest defender may block the shot from behind.

7. Cutting

a. Work on defending the flex cut by riding or chucking the cutter and influencing his path over the top and have the screener's man bump, if necessary. Then stop the screener from stepping or ducking in and posting up.

   b. Bump and chuck cutters after they pass the ball. Ride cutters in the direction you desire.

   c. Force and ride the cutter high or low. Have a rule stipulating what to do if he goes high or low. Decide if you want to bump, help or switch.

   d. Stay level with the ball when playing weakside cutters. Use the ball-you-man principle. Bump and force them away from where they want to go. Force them to cut behind and/or away from the ball.

   e. Practice defending and taking away weakside cuts. Take two steps down and two steps in the direction of the pass once the ball is in the air.

   f. Closely trail the man curling on the baseline turnout on the strong side of the court. Have the screener's defender step out and bump the curling player.

8. Trapping

   a. The nearest man to the ball can double the dribbler from behind if he turns his back.

   b. Weakside defenders must be alert to pick up the dive man if their men are trapping.

   c. When trapping the low post off of the passer cutting from the wing, the trapper must take the cutter below the post man before coming back to trap to seal the penetrating pass or drive to the goal.

   d. Practice and break down trapping the wing pick-and-roll. Practice the weakside rotation in this situation, especially the rotation if the ball is thrown over the weakside defender's head.

Defensively, move on the pass, not the catch.

9. Post Defense

   a. Have a rule for defending the pinch post.

   b. Have a rule for defending the step-up transition pick-and-roll.

   c. Establish how you want to defend the low post.

10. Talk

   a. Let the point guard know he is alone on a flat 1-4.

   b. Let defensive players know if they are "iced" out defensively or if the area behind them is empty.

   c. Talk on the pick-and-roll to permit the dribblers to know where the screen will be set.

Last-quarter defensive mentality should be to limit opponents to four one-shot fouls and permit no offensive rebounds.

Full-Court Pressure Defensive Rules

1. Pressure to change the game's tempo, to build for future use and to see how your opponent handles pressure.

2. Directly after a score and steal when pressuring, "multiply" by continuing immediate full-court pressure denial to create another scoring opportunity.

3. Decide if the strategy you want to use would be to execute one trap, and if this doesn't result in recovering the ball, you retreat back into normal man-to-man defense. We explain this as the "one-and-done" principle. You can also continue to pressure and trap until the play is over.

4. When using the 2-1-2 full-court press, the middle man presses and traps with the wing behind him if the pass is over his head and with the wing in front of him if the pass is in front of him.

5. Each individual trapping player must know how quick he is and how far from his man he can reasonably go to trap and still recover to place concentrated pressure on the trapped opponent. A good rule of thumb some coaches use is not to trap until you are within six feet of the man you are going to trap. This distance may vary depending on the quickness and skill of the trapping player.

6. The anticipator or interceptor should read the man being trapped (where he is facing) to help him look for the steal or step into the passing lane.

7. When trying to corral a dribbler who has beaten you, release and run to a spot in front of him or chase and try to tip the dribble from behind. Establish your rule beforehand so each defensive player knows how to react in this instance.

8. Trap from behind as you level with the ball if the man you are defending trails the play. Keep the ball out of the middle and force sideline.

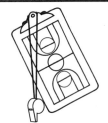

Look to "multiply" a breakaway basket or layup after a steal by immediately applying full-court pressure to get another quick score.

Defending the man with the ball

Good offensive players will get into a triple-threat position, enabling them to dribble, pass or shoot immediately upon receiving the ball. To take away that threat, most coaches want defenders to pressure the man with the ball to cause the offensive man to react to the defender instead of the opposite reaction. We want the defender to dictate the action. We teach making contact and pressuring the ball handler with your forearm. We don't want to give the offensive player a clear path to the basket for him to drive. We don't want to give him an uncontested shot, and we don't want to allow him to make an easy entry pass. To stop him effectively, we need to pressure and contain the man with the ball by using our hands and feet quickly and aggressively. We want to make the offensive player a dribbler, but don't want to let him penetrate. Again, teach your players to use their forearms.

We think you have to instruct your players to try and recognize an opposing player's tendencies. If he has a weak hand, we may want them to force him to use it. If his shooting range is inside 15 feet, we might want to drop off him a bit until he is 20 feet from the basket or pressure him early to keep him out of his range. We try not to let him become comfortable in the offensive end.

We maintain pressure. If the player still has the dribble alive, we don't want to get beat on the drive. If he has used up the dribble, then we get all over him so he doesn't have an open shot and the passing lanes are clogged.

The next step is determining how you want to play the baseline dribble drive and from where the help should come. We have decided we will trap the baseline drive with our defensive post man who hopefully will be fronting the low post while our three other defenders will rotate in a predetermined manner or by having the nearest defender not guarding the ball trap the dribbler.

Defending the man with the ball
(Dribbler and shooter, full-court, one-on-one drill)

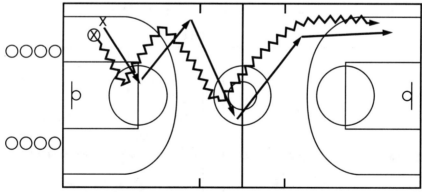

The player with the ball begins at the baseline and tries to beat his defender as the defender pressures and overplays, making him constantly change direction by getting his body and inside hand outside the dribbler. By doing this, we turn the dribbler and put ourselves in a position to steal the ball with our inside hand and body, stepping through and sealing the defender as we go for the ball.

We only look to steal if we have a clear shot at the ball. Our goal is to constantly turn the dribbler, forcing him to cross over, use up time and possibly turn the ball over. Once over midcourt, we channel the dribbler to the nearest sideline and deny penetration toward the middle as we play live one-on-one basketball. We are also working at not permitting the offense to reverse the ball. The drill ends once a basket is scored or the defense recovers the ball via a turnover or rebound. If the defender steals the ball, he tries to score against the offensive

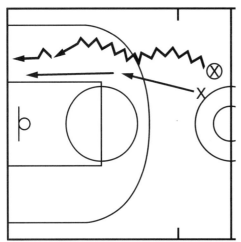

player who has just lost the ball. Players rotate from offense to defense to the end of the line. We don't want to allow the offense to beat us sideline or baseline.

A drill variation (left) is one-on-one half court with the same rules applying, except that the defensive man must "stop" the offensive player. If the offensive player scores, the defender must play the next offensive player. We alternate sides of the court in both drills as we do in all of our practices. A player stays on defense until he stops the offense and doesn't permit an offensive rebound.

Defending a shooter and dribbler

(Two stations)

Three players each pass a ball to an offensive player set to shoot with his dribble used. They run at him under control with their hand raised and jump, trying to alter his shot. We do not want to foul. In Diagram B, the dribble is now alive and the offensive player dribbles and the defender must deny penetration, stop the dribbler and pressure the shot with his hand raised. Once the shot is taken in both of the drills, the defender boxes out and makes contact. We don't rebound the ball to ensure that no one gets hurt. We alternate shooting the ball.

(A)   **(B)**

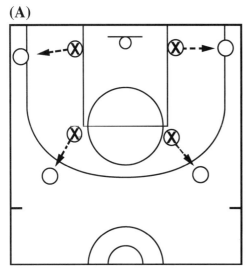 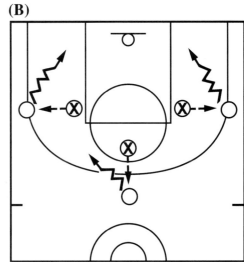

Defending the Dribbler or Passer

With the dribble alive, we force the offensive player sideline or middle, but stop his penetration by getting in front on him and forcing him away from the goal. Once we stop his dribble, we belly up to him with our hands raised to stop him from having a clear lane in which to deliver the ball. We also have the defensive player yell "deny," "pressure", etc., to let his teammates know the dribble is dead and that they must overplay and deny all outlets.

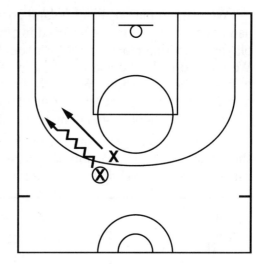

Defending a Player Without the Ball

(One-on-one wing overplay, two stations)

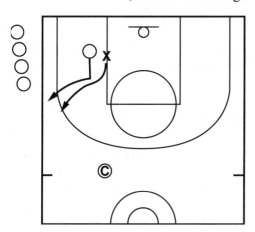 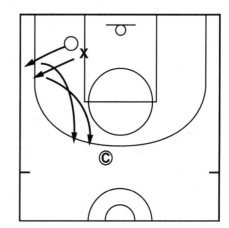

A coach or player passes the ball at each station (one station works the left side of the court at one basket and the other works the right side at the other basket).

We begin by overplaying one penetrating pass away in the ball-you-man principle (**B-Y-M**) on the low block and the offensive player then can pop to the wing, post up, curl, run up to the pinch post or loop to the top to receive the ball. The passer can pass as soon as the offensive player is free or wait until all options have been defended. Once the pass is made, the defender forces the offensive man sideline and baseline and cuts him off, denying a drive to the goal.

Defending the shooter

We want to put our hand up and contest every shot. Even if we don't get a hand on the ball, we might succeed in altering the shot. We need to know what a player's shooting range or comfort zone is and then force him out of that zone. We want to make the shooter dribble (but not allow him to penetrate). If he's dribbling, he can't shoot. We try to force good shooters to pass the ball, and we also concentrate on not leaving our feet on ball fakes. Decide if you want to "marry" good shooters and deny them the ball completely.

If a player does get a shot, we want to make sure we box him out after the shot. The shooter is probably the most dangerous rebounder on the floor. He usually is the first to know if the shot is going to miss and where it will bounce.

Run out on good shooters to break their concentration and to stop them from going to the offensive boards.

Defending the dribbler or passer

We must keep him in front of us to stop penetration. We force him to our help, sideline or baseline and then cut him off and make him pick up his dribble. We try to dictate what we want the offensive player to do. Make him react to us, not us to him. Each coach must decide which philosophy to embrace and then teach it to his players as a team defensive rule.

Once the man picks up his dribble, the best thing a defender can do is to pressure up on him making it difficult for him to pass. Use one's hands to block his line of vision and make it difficult for him to pass effectively. This helps our teammates and helps us emphasize that we all have a responsibility to help one another!

Defending a man without the ball

If you are one pass away, our basic principle is ball-you-man. You always want to be between the ball and your man and we want you to see your man and the ball. Your team philosophy is important here. Do you deny all passes with the dribble alive when one pass away or do you only deny the penetrating, rather than the lateral pass? We want to concentrate on aggressively clogging the passing lanes. We want to make ourselves as large as possible — stretch out our arms and legs to make it as difficult as possible for an opponent to complete a pass that is penetrating by being level with the ball.

Our players must instantly realize if they are one, two or three passes away. Are they guarding a man in position to receive a lateral pass or a penetrating pass? How good a shooter is the man you are defending? Have them factor this in when deciding how much help they can give.

They must put themselves in position to always see the ball and the man they are guarding. It's really important to see the ball at all times, not only defensively. A good rule to remember is that the ball will always take you to your man if you have lost him. Keep your eye on the ball and retreat to the goal until you find your man. This is a rule used by coaches teaching combination defense, and it is well served in man-to-man defensive concepts. Try to have your weakside defenders be in a line with the ball and the basket when they help defensively. Set up a drill to work on this principle and teach your players to move back and in the direction of the pass as the ball is in the air.

Drop to the level of the ball. If we are guarding someone at the top of the key and he passes to a wing and stays, then we drop to the free-throw line, keeping our man and the ball in sight. If the wing picks up his dribble, then we quickly deny the passing lane back to our man. NBA rules don't permit this because of the illegal defense rules, but this still enables us to teach our players how we want them to react once the pass is in the air. This concept will definitely work where zone rules are not in effect.

We teach our players that they should "move on the pass, not on the catch." You can gain an advantage of a couple of steps in the proper direction while the ball is in the air. We don't want to wait until the pass is completed to react. Coaches also have to decide how to play cutters without the ball. Do you bump or chuck them and/or force them to take a path you predetermine? We work very hard on stepping back and in the direction of the ball when working on eliminating an inside cut to the ball from the strong or weak side.

Shell Drill

The Shell Drill on the half court can teach your players to cover almost every defensive situation or maneuver. It can be done with three offensive and three defensive players or more commonly with four against four. You can set it up with a one-guard or two-guard front. We begin at a controlled pace, work up to half speed and then go full speed. You can substitute or add a coach as a passer to create more intensity and defensive movement, having the offense now play with an extra man.

Align offensive players in an arc, about 20 to 25 feet from the basket. You can use the three-point line as your guide. Give one player the ball and make each of the defenders move into his proper position in relation to the ball each time the ball is passed. Have the offensive player dribble once or twice and then pick up the ball. How do the defenders react? Make a simple lateral guard-to-guard pass. How does that affect the defenders? After making several guard-to-guard or guard-to-forward passes, make some skip passes. Begin to have offensive players exchange positions after a pass. Have offensive players cut to the basket. Have the next offensive player replace the cutter and set a screen on the ball. Work to help and recover to stop dribble penetration. Explain how you want to play the guard-to-guard pass and then the guard-to-forward pass and how you want the defensive players to react in each instance.

During the course of the drill, every player can learn to react to every possible maneuver by the offense. This is when and how you can establish your defensive rules. There are a limited number of offensive maneuvers a player can take on a basketball court, and you must teach a defensive counter for each of those actions. Only by establishing a philosophy of defense and through the repetition of drills can you get your players to react instinctively to all situations.

No matter what level you coach, you should spend time nearly every day teaching the Shell Drill to emphasize basic defensive movement and principles.

Support Defense Explanation

(One station, four-man Shell Drill setup, no dribble permitted)

The defender guarding the ball pressures the offensive player. All the other defenders not one penetrating pass away, slough off the ball in a line with the ball and the basket once the pass is in the air. A player one penetrating pass away with the dribble alive must pressure and deny the ball. He also tries to force the receiver to receive the passer higher up on the floor and further away from the basket. We pass the ball every two seconds to another offensive player as the defenders:

    a. Pressure and deny the pass.

    b. Rotate and move in the direction of the pass.

    c. Get level with the ball and in a line with the ball and the basket.

Once the coach yells "play," the dribble is alive and we play basketball until a score or stop. We rotate from offense to defense to a new offensive group.

Shell Defense Support Drill

(A)

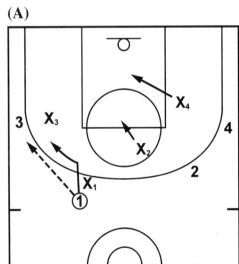

(B)

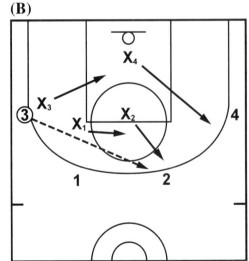

On the penetrating pass from 1 to the overplayed and pressured 3, X1 immediately drops down level with the ball to deny 3's penetration to the lane as X3 takes away the baseline and forces 3 toward the help from X1. X2 and X4 drop down to help from the weak side, level with the ball and the basket.

3 passes over X1 to 2. X2 reacts and moves to pressure the ball. X1 and X3 move in the direction of the pass, level with the ball and the basket and X4 moves to overplay and deny 4 the penetrating pass from 2 to the wing position.

Shell Defense Support Drill

(C)

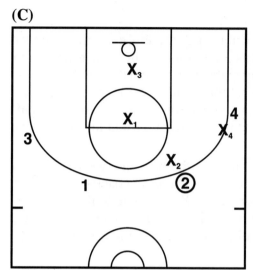

(D)

2 has the basketball and all defensive players have the reverse responsibilities that they had in Diagram A.

Diagram B is mirrored here on the opposite side of the court.

Shell Defense Support Drill

All drills begin without a post man whom we normally play man-to-man in our regular defensive scheme.

Support Phase: Move on the pass in the direction of the pass with the man guarding the ball pressuring his opponent. Ball-you-man (B-Y-M) principle with the defender one pass away denying the pass. Players off the ball are in position to help with their rule being that they should be seeing the ball and positioning themselves in a line with the ball and the basket.

With the ball on the wing, the same rules apply. The coach must decide if he wants to pressure the man with the ball sideline, force him to the middle or simply have him keep his man in front of him. Other men slough to the ball and get level with the ball to jam the driving and passing lanes. We want to force the man to pass back outside. In the drill, the ball is passed every two seconds to see how players: a) Move on the pass; b) Move in the direction of the pass (two steps back and one in the direction of the pass); c) Pressure the ball and close out on their men; d) Deny and overplay if one pass away in a penetrating position; e) Weakside players are in the lane and level with or below the ball; f) On a forward-to-guard pass we try to stop ball reversal by having the guard's defender pressure his man to force the ball back to the player who just passed the ball.

We will then add cutters replacing each other, guards crossing with or without the ball, switching, inverting the weakside guards and forwards, interchange and taking away the cutter's inside cut. We will make major or minor adjustments during the season when we prepare to defend an outstanding individual player, but our basic rules of defense do not vary. We believe strongly in sticking to what we practice and preach.

Shell Defense
(Help and recover)

In Diagram A, to step in and help stop dribble penetration, each player moves down and level in the direction of the ball as penetration occurs. The nearest man to the dribbler stops penetration by getting in the passing and driving lane, causing the dribbler to stop or to pass over the helping man's outside shoulder. We do not want to permit dribble penetration nor a penetrating pass towards the goal. We also want the offensive players without the ball to move and fake to disconcert their individual defenders.

In Diagram B, on dribble penetration toward the baseline, we want X4 to cross the lane and stop penetration to the basket, X2 to rotate back to the basket for weak side help and the weakside rebound and X1 to rotate to the middle of the lane just below the foul line to play both guards in the perimeter area and stop all passes into the lane. X3 chases the ball to trap and seal the dribbler or shut down the foul lane area.

In Diagram C, rotation pass thrown back to G2 from F3, X1 covers G2. He gets the free man in the direction of the help. X3 denies F4, X4 helps in the lane and X2 recovers to the middle of the free-throw line and plays G1. (This stops penetration and weak side cuts to the goal.)

Diagram D shows our positions when G2 dribble penetrates the middle.

Shell Defense
(Help and recover)

(A)

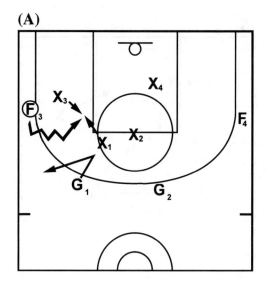

(B)

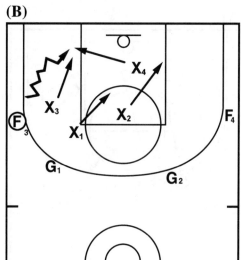

(C)

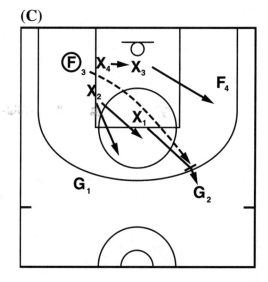

(D)

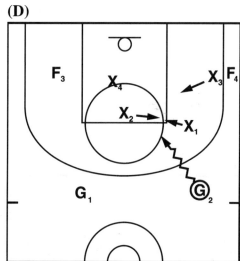

Defensive Support Drill and Shell Defense

All drills are run without a post man, because we normally begin by playing the post man straight man-to-man.

(A)

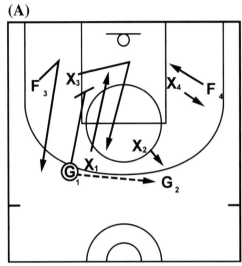

(B)

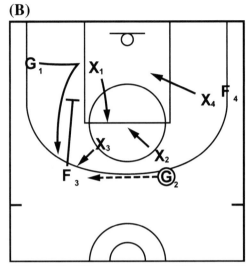

Guard-to-guard pass and interchange or pindown. No dribble permitted.

G2 to F3. We can switch X1 and X2 when their men cross with or without the ball, but we do this as a game adjustment, not early in our drilling. Here X3 closes out on the ball. X1 overplays G1 on the wing and X2 steps back and in the direction of the pass as does X4, and X2 lets X4 slide through as G2 pins down on F4.

(C)

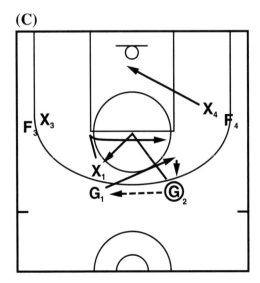

(D)

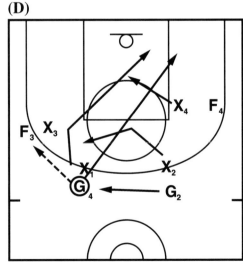

Shell Drill

(Guard-to-guard pass and interchange or pindown)

We begin the drill by permitting no dribbles which encourages a quick reaction to each pass that is made.

In Diagram A, on a pass from G1 to G2, X1 releases down and in the direction of the ball as G1 cuts vertically and sets a screen for F3. This permits X3 to slide or step up and inside G1 to cover the passing lane to F3 should G2 reverse the ball instead of passing to F4 on the wing. We want to slide through one man removed with the ball on the other side of the court on a vertical screen. We also always want to pressure the passer. Another advantage of using the Shell Drill is that it also enables each defensive player to learn to defend players in any position in the offensive end of the court.

In Diagram B, we also run this drill with the guard-to-guard pass and backscreens and we caution the backscreener's defender not to chase and get too close to the picker, thus screening his own teammate, which would permit a lob pass inside for the offensive player receiving the backpick. At some point we explain that at times we will switch weak side guard/forward exchanges or invert to keep our big man closer to the goal. That's not a definite rule, but a special situation adjustment we can and do make when facing a specific opponent.

In Diagram C, on a guard-to-forward pass and horizontal exchange (G to G) opposite the pass, guards should slide through one man removed and keep defending their own man. Again, at times in game situations we have adjusted our thinking and put in a rule permitting our guards to switch whenever the opposing guards cross with or without the ball.

In Diagram D, G to F pass and cut through with the other guard replacing. Players again have the opportunity to play all four defensive positions. The defense off the ball must step down and in the direction of the pass to get level with the ball.

After awhile we can invert and switch weakside high/low interchange to keep the big man home as per our trapping rotation.

Shell Drill
(Guard-to-Forward pass and cut-through with other guard replaced)

(A)

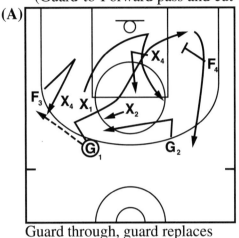

Guard through, guard replaces

In Diagram B, we have the G to F pass and cut to the goal with the replacing guard setting a screen on the ball (or Diagram D), the weakside forward setting a screen on the ball across the court as the weakside guard fakes to the ball and goes away on a counter move. The man with the ball is taught not to dribble until the screen is set so as to avoid an offensive foul call by the official. Coaches can also cover defending the loop out front or a guard burying to the corner in this drill.

(B)

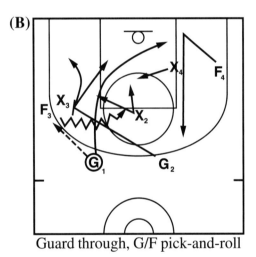

Guard through, G/F pick-and-roll

(C)

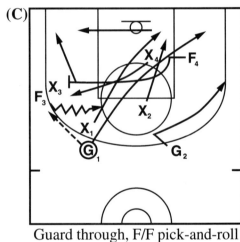

Guard through, F/F pick-and-roll

(D)

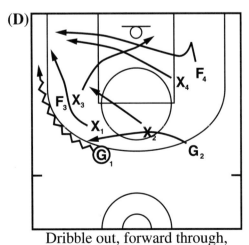

Dribble out, forward through, guard replaces

(E)

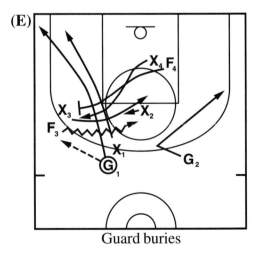

Guard buries

Shell Drill
(Guard-to-Forward)

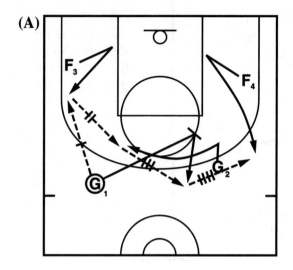

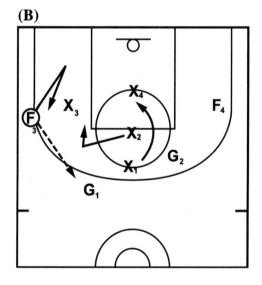

Shell Drill

A. Guard-to-forward, basket or lane cut and pindown as F3 passes to G2 who has replaced G1 after G1 has cut. X1 tries to go over or through the screen and he trails, if possible on the curl

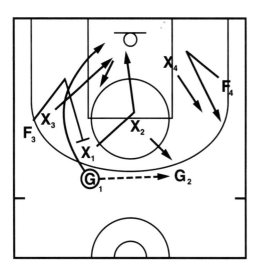

B. Guard1 to Guard 2, blind pig back-pick by F3 for G1 after the pass has been made to G2. X3 is responsible for helping X1. X3 must therefore not chase the backpicker, F3.

Defensive Assignments

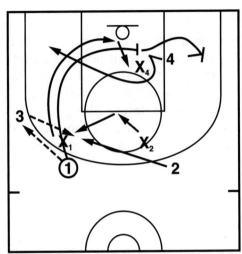 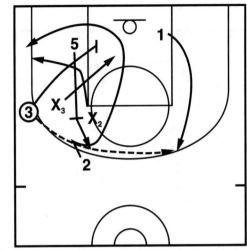

Guard to forward, screen across after cut and then UCLA upblock on the strong side for replacing guard. Pin down for cutter on the weak side of F/G2 on strong side if G1 replaces on the perimeter.

(A) **(B)**

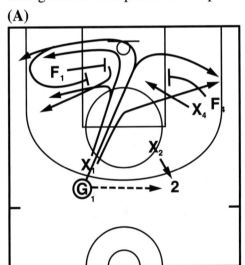 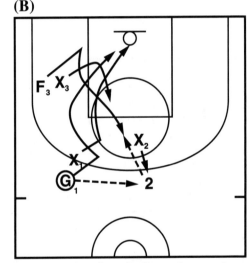

In A, a guard-to-guard pass and lane cut to the basket for pindown from wings on either side. The guard may also set up a curl action here or he can curl and pick his teammate's defender. How do you defend this? We set it up and practice it.

In B, a guard-to-guard pass with blind pig action (post flash to set up a backdoor play). To demonstrate defensive help rotation off the ball and rotation against the flash post. X3 must not chase the back screener. The coach must decide if X1 bellies up to G1 and goes over the screen or steps to the ball on the screen and cuts inside to the goal. He must see the ball. We have to call out the screen and pressure the ball. We could also switch or squeeze the backpick as we do in the dribble handoff defense as long as we talk and communicate.

61

Defensive Assignments

(C)

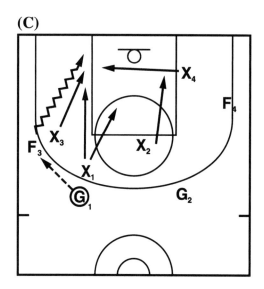

In C, guard-to-forward pass, baseline drive and double from the top and sending the weakside forward across the lane and having the weakside guard drop back to defend the goal. The strongside post offensive player should step up the lane as a passing outlet.

(D1)   **(D2)**

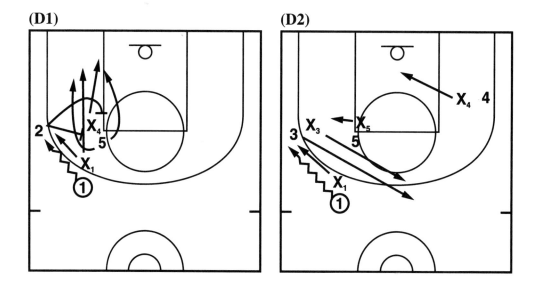

In D1, the guard dribbles the forward out to set a screen either high or low on the post man or (D2) the forward can also loop up to clear out an area for the dribbler. Help there must come from the weak side.

Shell Drill

(A)

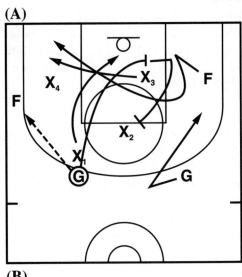

A. G to F, pass and cut

B. Defensive assignments. We can switch X1 and X2 on the weak side away from the ball by having a rule that you can switch equals and also by trying to keep the bigger defensive player on the weak side, closer to the goal.

C. G to F, screen across into UCLA upblock

D. G to F pass, baseline drive

E. G dribbles wing out

(B)

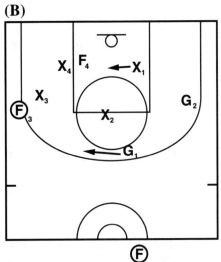

(C)

(D)

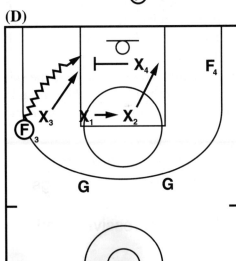

(E)

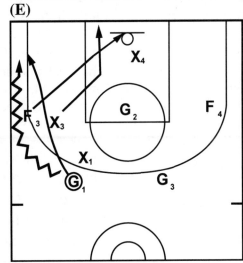

Defensive help and the rotation off the ball

How do you rotate during certain situations if you are playing off of the ball? What are your responsibilities on the weak side defensively in covering isolations, doubling the post, fronting the post, rotating against the lob, doubling the baseline drive, helping defend the high-low lob play, the screen across the lane, splitting the post and/or back door or blind pig maneuvers?

Individual post defense

The first step is determining how you want to play the post player before he has the ball. Do you want to play in front of him, behind him or three-quarter wrap around him? Do you want to push him off the block? Do you want to take away his spot by meeting him higher up the floor before he has an opportunity to establish his most comfortable position? How are you going to play him once he gets the ball? How do you play him with the ball in the corner as opposed to the ball on the wing? Do you want to face-guard and play belly-to-belly in height disadvantage mismatch situations?

Sometimes you may feel you don't want to defend the low post in the normal or accepted manner. Don't worry about that. Do what you think will work for you and your team, even if it is unorthodox. You may catch opponents unprepared. As long as each of your players realizes his responsibilities everyone is on the same page.

Set up individual drills to show the defender how to use leverage and quickness to prevent the offensive player from getting where he wants to go. Bodycheck him. Chuck him. Ride him over or under. Step in his path and force him to go around you. If one of your assistants is a big man, utilize him to explain the nuances of post play.

How do you play a mismatch? You might want to always front the post in that situation. It forces your opponents to make a great pass, but you must pressure the passer to help the defender in the mismatch. You're making your opponent fight you to get post position. He might get called for an offensive foul or give up when it becomes too physical for him to get open. Explain how to sit on a player's legs when fronting him. You must help the mismatched player by putting extra pressure on the ball so it becomes more difficult to change sides with the ball, set up a lob pass or lock-and-lob situation.

What do you want the weakside defender to do? You need help if the defender is sealed off. How does the fronting post defender react when there is dribble penetration from a guard? Does he have the confidence to attack the dribbler knowing that his back is covered?

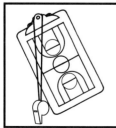

In our drills we constantly encourage and almost force our players to execute things correctly. We want them to run wide, spread the floor, defend aggressively and always concentrate.

Rules for Defending Post Players and the Low Post

1. Meet the man early to keep him off the block and take away comfortable post position.

2. Play on the ball side and three-quarter the low post. Use your body and forearm to push the offensive player off the block.

3. To front from three-quarter position, use your forearm and step over the front leg of the offensive player to move him off the block.

4. When fronting the post, lean and sit on the offensive player's legs and move your feet and the man with your hands up in front of you.

5. When playing behind the post, push him out, keep moving and make and break contact to keep the offensive player busy and off-balance.

6. Use your hands to deflect passes into the post while you keep moving so the offensive player doesn't know which side you're on.

7. Bump the cutter before he can establish post position.

8. Don't front the post too high with no weakside help.

9. Face-guard, belly-to-belly, hands up. Encourage and force an offensive foul.

10. When fronting the post, you must signal the man playing the passer to pressure the ball aggressively.

11. Brace and step back when playing or sealed behind extremely strong post players. Make them lose their balance when contact is broken or turn and look for you thereby losing sight of the ball.

Pick-and-roll defense

You can use colors, names or signals to trigger your specific pick-and-roll defenses, i.e. squeeze or hug, hedge, bump the screener into the defender off the dribble, through, over, hard show or double-team.

What is your rotation on step-out (wing pick-and-roll)? Do you want the weakside low man to come across or would you prefer the weakside high defender to trap?

Explain how you zone up off the ball and zone the top, middle and basket positions.

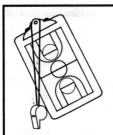
Stay at home and lock in on good shooters with the clock running down or when your team is in a trapping mode.

Team post defense

What rules do you have for the rest of the team when the ball does go into the post? Do you want to double-team? Where does that double-team come from? Do you want to come from behind the post player? Do you want to do it with another big man or a smaller, quicker player? Do you want to try to block the shot from behind? If the dribble is used up, do you drop off the double-team or add more pressure to the passer? When do you double? On the pass? On the dribble?

These are some of the many questions you have to answer and should make a part of your philosophy. You have to learn to adjust depending on that day's opposition. There might be certain players that you want to immediately double in the post and others you'd prefer to have the ball. You have to develop drills to work on this, and practice them every day.

Defending the baseline drive

Do you want to help from the weak side, fake and recover, release and beat the dribbler to the spot, try to steal or slap the dribble from behind or automatically trap the baseline drive with a specific player (the nearside post man or next nearest player)?

Doubling the Baseline Drive
(Three-on-three half-court drill with two stations)

(A)   **(B)**

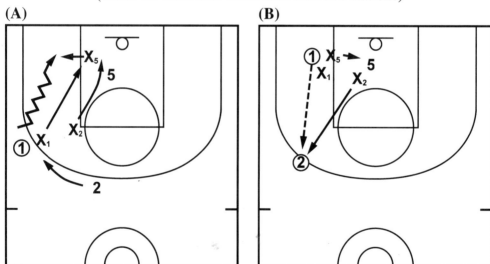

We force the dribbler sideline and baseline as we front the low post with X5 and sag down level with the ball off X2. If X1 is beaten, the nearest man traps the dribbler. In this case X5 traps and X2 rotates back to the goal to take and box 5. X1, who has pressured the dribbler, is now responsible for sealing the middle. He bellys-up and doubles with X5 as he forces the dribbler by toward the middle. X2 must level with the ball and protect the basket. He rotates out if a pass is made back outside to 2 on his side of the court. We play help defense by rotating and taking the free man in the direction of the help. X2 must recognize his own ability and that of his opponent in determining how far down he must go to prevent a pass to 5 from 1. We want to make the offense take the lower percentage shot.

Defensive Drills
(3-on-3, half-court)

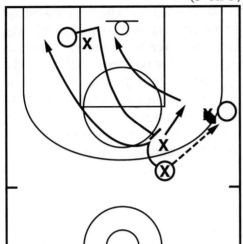

Point-to-wing pass with weakside backpick. The defender on passer must step down and in the direction of the pass. The defender of the screener must bump or chuck the man being screened. He cannot chase and get too close to his man and screen his own teammate.

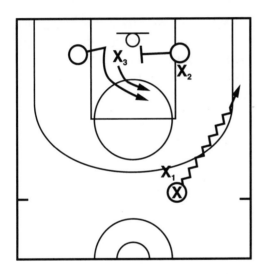

Dribble to the wing, setting up a screen across, if no post man is available. X3 must ride his man up the lane or stay attached and force him to the baseline. We prefer the former.

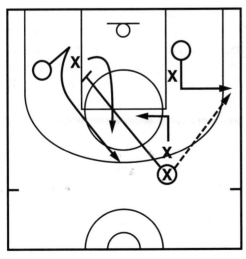

A pass from the guard to the wing and the guard cuts away to screen the weakside low post. We want the defense on the weakside post to slide up the lane and shoot the gap, rather than follow or trail his man.

Defensive Drills
(3-on-3, half-court)

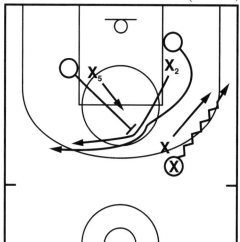

Dribble to the wing and low wing man on strong side loops up and gets blind counter backscreen from the weakside low post man. X2 can body up and fight over the screen. X5 might want to screen his opponent, permitting X2 to go under the screen. Here we show X2 stepping over the screen by making himself thinner.

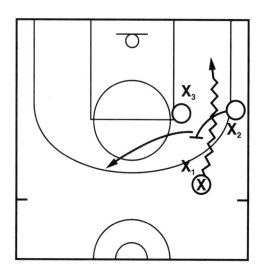

Step-up screen for dribbler with the high post counter on the wing overplay. We must have the back defenders talking to alert X1. In this case we might establish a rule enabling us to switch this maneuver.

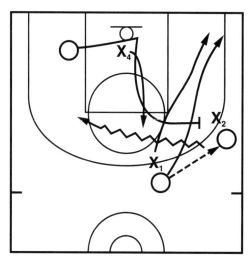

Point pass and bury. The weakside post comes up to set a pick. We must hard show and get over or trap and double the dribbler and the defender in the corner, X1, must pick up the roll man unless we are coming from the weak side of the floor to help.

Defensive Drills
(3-on-3, half-court)

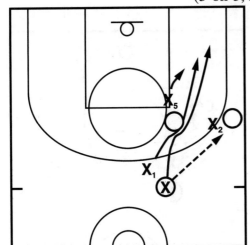

UCLA cut. Ride the point over the screen as the post defender steps to the ball side to help. He must watch his man going backdoor so it is best that he steps out on an angle to help.

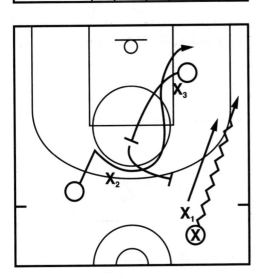

Defending Hawk Diagonal Cut on a dribble to the wing. X2 must ride the cutter off the post as X3 talks and calls out the screen and X1 forces the dribbler to the corner.

3-on-3
(Half-court)

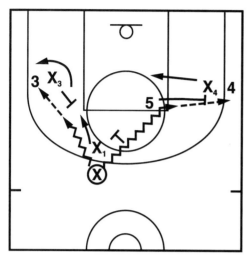

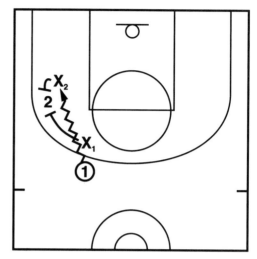

A. Defend the penetrate-and-pitch. Run under control in front of the men, not at the ball.

B. Trap the dribble handoff and weave.

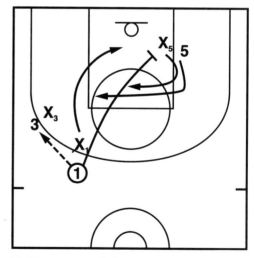

C. High pick-and-roll. Rotate from the weakside baseline to pick up the roll man.

D. Pass, cut, pick.

4-on-4
(Half-court)

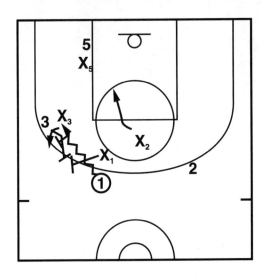

A. Attack the post on passes inside.

B. Trap the dribble handoff (six feet away). On the handoff from 1 to 3, X1 jumps out to double 3 with X3.

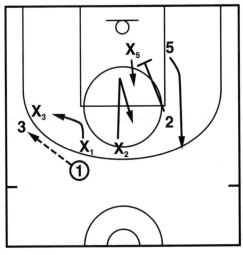

C. Weakside defense invert (keep the big man at home). X2 goes halfway down as 2 screens down on 5. 5 calls the switch and we keep our big man home on the weak side.

Defending a screen

Photo©Frank McGrath

Team Defenses

You have to determine if you want to have full-court pressure, three-quarter-court pressure, half-court pressure or perimeter pressure. Do you want to let them get the ball in after a basket or are you going to pressure the entire floor? Do you trap the first pass? Many times your personnel determines which philosophy you use. You might want to pressure only the guards and use a big man to help out on a double-team. You have to set up drills to cover all the situations you might face or wish to employ.

You may decide you want to teach to switch only equal-sized players or unequal as well. If you're the first big man back on defense, you are responsible for taking the first big man who comes down the floor. You have to help and talk and communicate. The more often you go over these situations in practice and develop drills to practice them, the better you will handle them in a game.

Decide and list which defenses to play based on your personnel and then set up, teach and practice them. You never really know when you might need a new defense in a particular game. Practice one or more. Be prepared should the need arise.

Full-Court Defenses

1. Man-to-man

2. Zone

3. Combination man-to-man and zone

Full-Court Press Defense
(Trapping from in front or from behind)

Rules:

1. Depending upon who we play and what defense we are using, we decide to either pressure or not pressure the inbounds passer.

2. We trap the first pass and then have the remaining three players zone by:

   a. Covering the near sideline

   b. Covering the middle

   c. Our deep man covers the basket

(In this scheme A and B are almost in man-to-man defense.)

3. As soon as a pass is made out of the trap and over the trappers, the men in the first trap or any trap go back level with or in front of the ball and now they are almost in a man-to-man.

4. If the pass out of the trap is back, we are still in our zone.

5. In face guard denial, we don't play the inbounder, but we have a man advantage in denying the outlets the ball. We deny for three to four seconds and look to steal the ball.

6. We can, in essence, go zone, man-to-man and zone on the same possession.

7. If we steal the ball and score, we want to immediately pressure again to "multiply" the score or steal and score again.

8. The man covering the basket must see the ball and cover the goal first. He has to be careful not to go for the steal too high, because if he doesn't make the steal, he'll give up an easy basket.

9. We may come on the dribble from in front in our run and jump defense.

10. If the player we are defending trails the ball, we can double the ball from the side or back, usually with the 4 or 5 man, but sometimes the 3.

11. We don't want the dribbler to beat us on the short sideline, because once he does, he can see the whole court perfectly and has a greater capacity to make a scoring pass with the numbers in his team's favor.

12. We want our defenders to set up on an angle so they can develop peripheral vision and see the whole court. It is almost the "V" in our ball-you-man principle. See the ball and your man.

Full-Court Press Defense
(Trapping from in front or from behind)

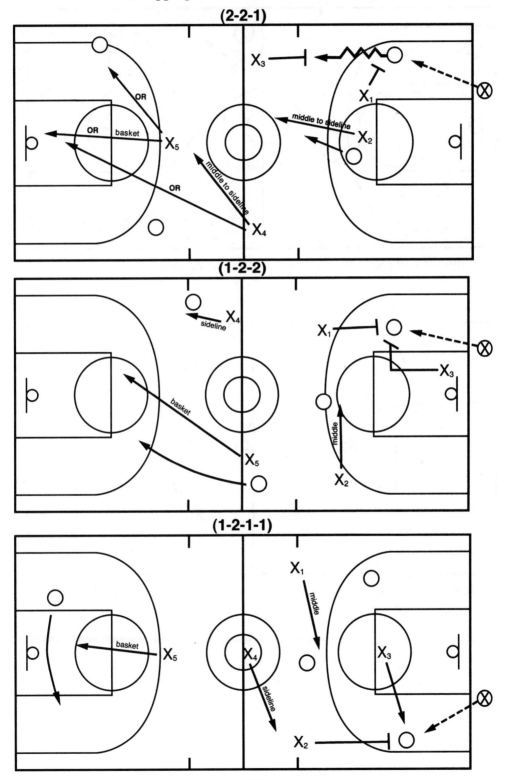

(2-2-1)

(1-2-2)

(1-2-1-1)

Full-Court Press Rules
(Zone, sideline, middle, basket)

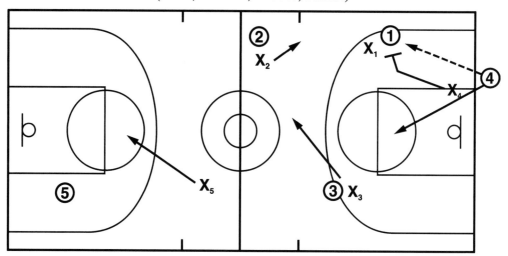

Trap the ball and if the pass is in front of you, zone.

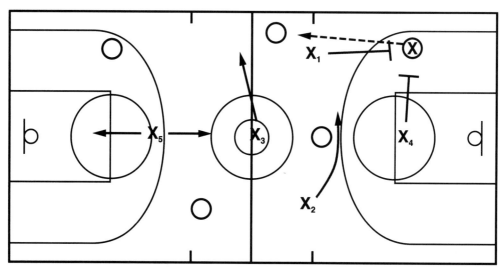

If the pass is over your head coming out of the trap, level back with the ball into man-to-man.

Full-Court Press Rules
(Zone, sideline, middle, basket)

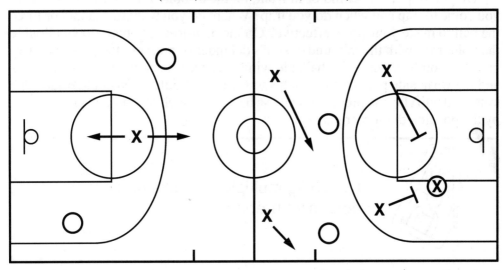

If the next pass comes back in front of you, return to the zone defense and try to trap the ball.

Half-court defenses

1. Man-to-man
2. Zone
3. Combination: Triangle-and-two, box- or diamond-and-one
4. Half-court trap
5. Matchup

Three-quarter-court defenses

1. Man-to-man
2. Zone
3. Combination
4. Trap
5. Run-and-jump

When defending a dribbler in the press, don't let him beat you on the short side of the court. Force him to the trapper. Don't permit him to see the entire court.

Half-court press/trap

Do you trap from behind or in front; on the dribble or the pass? How far do you come to trap and when do you trap? Where do you want to channel or force the ball to make your press effective? On the man-to-man press, do you double the point man with the inbound passer's defender or pressure the pass and face-guard the outlets, while the ballside wing defender steps up and fakes the trap and the weak side plays off and helps toward the middle? You could establish a system identifying the press you will use based on which of your players scores or by the position the scorer plays.

Coaching multiple offenses helps your defensive preparation.

Defending Some of the Plays Most Frequently Used in the NBA

Set up the offensive maneuver and then practice defending it.

1. Downscreen or pindown
2. Curl
3. Screen across the lane and rolling back to the ball
4. UCLA high post cut
5. Scissors or floppy — 2-3 cross in the lane out of double stack or single/double
6. Weakside cut
7. Pick-and-roll
   a. Center or middle
   b. Wing
   c. Corner
   d. Step up
   e. Pick and repick
   f. Loop
8. Perimeter interchange off of the ball
9. Flex cut
10. Split post
    a. Normal cross
    b. Blind backpick
11. Dribble handoff (weave action)
12. Backpick
13. Button hook in the post
14. Isolations
15. Counter or flare
16. Turnouts
17. Pick-the-picker
18. Screen down, post up and widen out
19. Triangle move (screen across and pin down on screener)
20. Slide through on diagonal big for small weakside pindown; push the screener
21. Zipper cut
22. Utah cut
23. Atlanta cut
24. Staggered screens
25. Counter off the zipper or dribble wing out and over entry

Defending Some of the Plays Most Frequently Used in the NBA
(Stations used in practice)

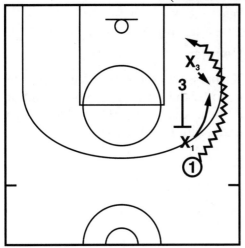

Step-up Pick and Roll

X3 must call out the screen and X1 must body up to the dribbler and get over the top with X3 stepping out to help and recover.

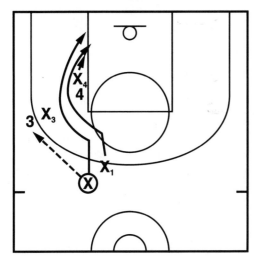

UCLA

X1 rides O1 over the top and inside X3 and X4. X4 softens to the ball to help X1, but he must not permit X4 to go to the goal.

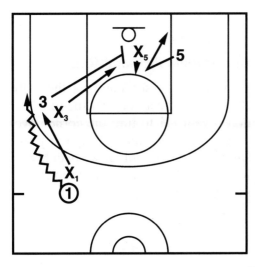

Screen Across and Fake

X1 pressures O1. X5 must stay attached to his man and ride him over the top of O3's screen. X3 helps and bumps O5 if he is ahead of X5 or if O5 goes baseline.

Defending Some of the Plays Most Frequently Used in the NBA
(Stations used in practice)

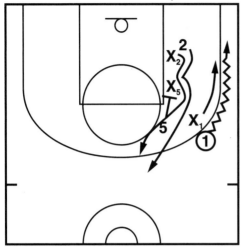

Counter

X1 pressures the ball. X2 tries to ride O2 over the screen as X5 helps and/or bumps. X5 may hug O5 and let X2 go under him to get to O2.

Staggered Screen

X1 pressures the ball. X2 rides O2 under each screen and X5 tries to bump O2 and X4 tries to hold his man and not let him screen. If we switch, we replace each other and switch up the line.

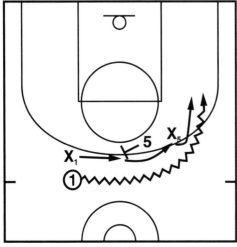

Center Field Pick-and-Roll

We want to hard show and trap this with X5 and X1 must get over the top. We don't want O1 to turn the corner. We would only go under if 1 is a poor shooter and then only if we decide beforehand not to try and fight over the screen.

Defending Some of the Plays Most Frequently Used in the NBA
(Stations used in practice)

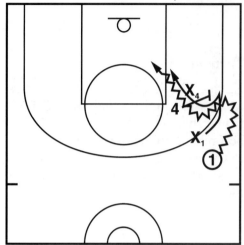

Wing Pick-and-Roll

We can force it sideline or trap with a hard show and over as in the previous diagram.

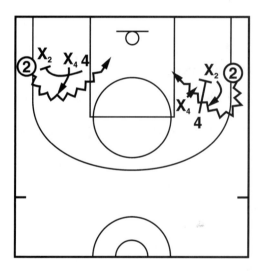

Corner Pick-and-Roll

We want to force middle and trap this with X4. We do not want the offense to turn the corner. X4 must step out and trap this early.

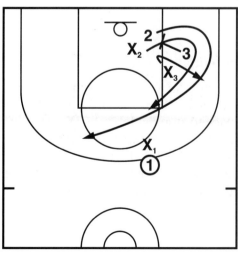

Curl

X2 must get to O2's outside shoulder and trail and get over O3's screen. X3 must bump and slow O2 and then get back to O3. It is also imperative that X1 pressure the ball.

81

Defending Some of the Plays Most Frequently Used in the NBA
(Stations used in practice)

Turnout

X2 rides O2's outside shoulder and tries to pressure him on the wing and X3 fronts the low post. We may decide beforehand to have X2 shoot the gap to try and steal the pass. If we do, X3 must protect in case of a backdoor move by 2 or 3.

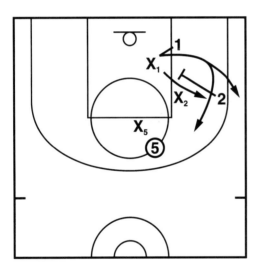

Downscreen

X2 is physical and tries to stop O2 from screening down. X5 pressures the pass and X1 rides O1 outside the screen or tries to shoot the gap. Your defensive philosophy dictates how you want to play this maneuver.

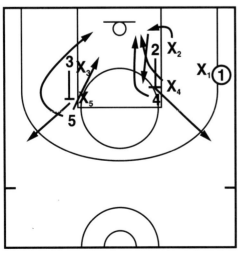

Upblock

X2 and X3 must talk and not chase screeners. They must help and give space to stop the lob pass. X5 goes inside to recover his man and X2 slows to stop the lob to O4 as X4 slides through. We would prefer X2 to come up inside 2 to deny him the ball.

Defending Some of the Plays Most Frequently Used in the NBA
(Stations used in practice)

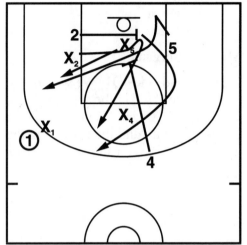

Pick-the-Picker

X5 pushes his man up toward the middle on O2's screen. X4 tries to stop O4 from screening down and X2 tries to get through inside X4 to get O2 coming up. The ball is on the other side of the court so X2 does not trail O2. If we know a team uses this option we might instruct X4 to screen 4 and not permit him to set the downscreen.

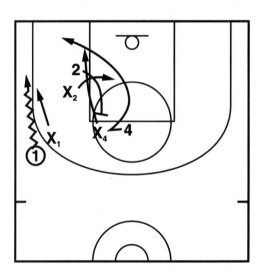

Utah Cut

X4 rides O4 over O2's back screen. X2 trails O2 to help for the lob and he must bump O4 if X4 is picked. X1 pressures 1 to make any pass difficult. When we add a fourth defender on the weak side he must be ready to rotate and stop the lob or lock-and-lob.

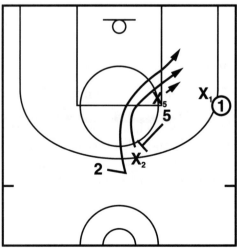

Atlanta (Hawk) Cut

X2 gets inside O2 and tries to get him off the block or he rides him over the screen by O5. X5 helps and bumps O2 on his cut if he goes behind 5. We would prefer X2 to body up and force 2 over 5 and toward the strongside corner.

Defending Some of the Plays Most Frequently Used in the NBA
(Stations used in practice)

Multiple Screens

X1 trails and rides O1. We would like him to force O1 over the screens. If not possible, X4, X5 and X3 must help stop O1 by bumping and then stopping the interior pass. We can also switch up the line.

Blind Misdirection

X3 can trail and ride O3 or get over the screen by X4. The perimeter players must help pressure the passers to help X3.

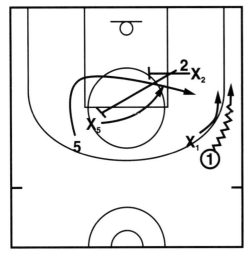

Diagonal

X2 must talk. X2 cannot chase the backpickcr. Hc must be in position to bump and slow him down. X5 must try to get up to and ride O5 over the screen. If not, he must take a shortcut and go over the top to beat him to the spot.

Defending Some of the Plays Most Frequently Used in the NBA
(Stations used in practice)

Single/Double

We want to force O2 only one way, taking away one side of the court. This decision must be established as a definite defensive rule. We may even decide to switch every 2/3 baseline cross.

Skip Pass (Backpick)

On the screen of X2 by O5, X5 must go to the corner to get O2 when he receives if X2 cannot get over the top and then X2 would seal 5.

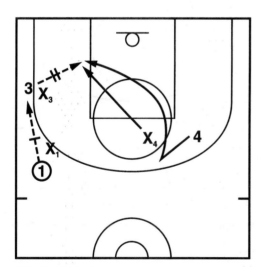

Weakside Cut

X4 must play B-Y-M and force O4 behind him. X4 must move level with the ball as the pass is in the air.

Flex Cut

We want X3 to bump and ride and force X3 over the screen. X5 helps, bumps and recovers to stop O5 from posting.

85

Defense — 2-on-2

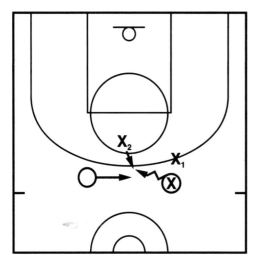

We go 2-on-2 from the top of the key. (Ball-you-man)

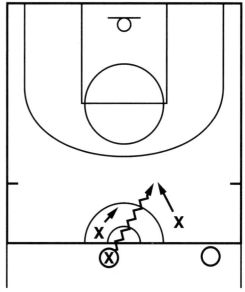

From above midcourt (Ball-you-man)

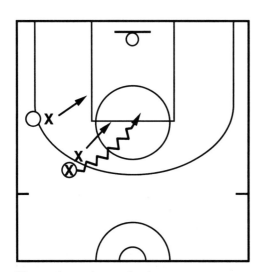

From the point and wing

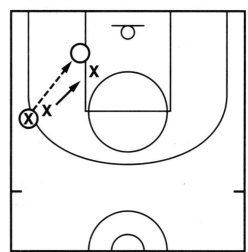

From the wing and post

Defense — 2-on-2

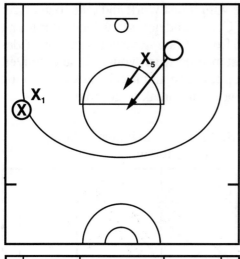

From the wing and weakside post, X5 must force the post player high.

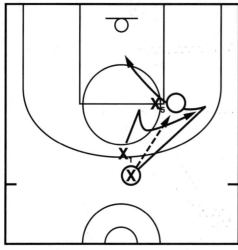

From the point and pinch or high post, X1 must take two steps down and two steps in the direction of the pass as soon as the ball leaves the ball handler's hands.

We also go 2-on-2 and defend all pick-and-roll and loop options. We vary these drills to get maximum defensive practice exposure.

When we work 5-on-5 half-court or full-court, we also want to practice all of our out-of-bounds plays from all areas of the court and at the same time work on our defensive out-of-bounds strategy and execution. This helps us prepare for all possible situations.

Defensive Drill
(1-on-1 wing overplay)

A coach or player passes the ball. The wing must work and fake to get free:
Options — A. Post Up; B. Pop Out; C. Cut up and across the lane after going down to the block; D. Pinch post; E. If fronted (step over outside leg of defender and get position); F. Close the distance between you and the defender, then break to get free; G. Take the man up the lane and break back door to the basket; H. Loop; I. Step, freeze the defender and break to get free

A. Walk the man down and pop out.

B. From the low post, fake up and pop to the wing.

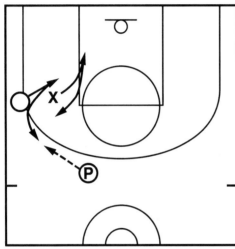

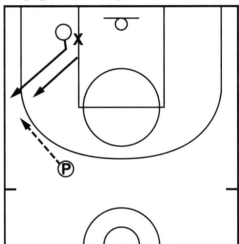

C. Walk the man up the lane, stop and pop out.

D. Fake up and go backdoor.

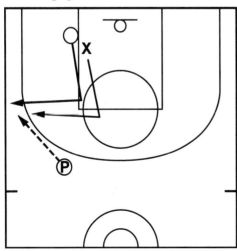

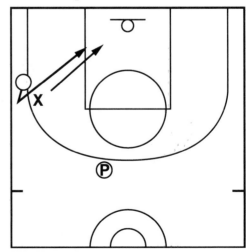

Defensive Drill
(1-on-1 Wing Overplay)

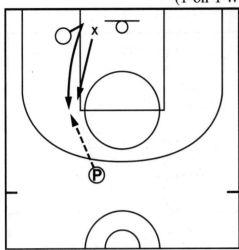

E. Break from the low post to the pinch post.

F. Take the defender to the lane and curl back to the corner.

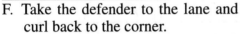

G. Fake down and loop across the top.

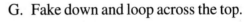

Defensive Drill
(1-on-1 from the top or corner)

A. We force left or right from the top and try to keep the offensive player out of the lane. (X1)

B. From the corner, we try to take away the baseline and force the player with the ball away from the goal and angle him out to the middle of the court and away from the basket. (X2)

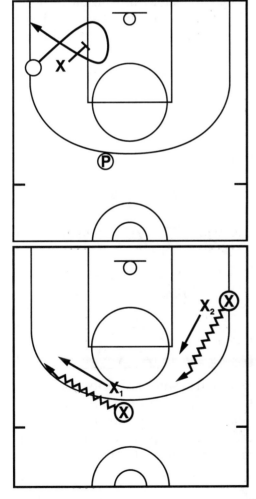

Examples of Defensive Drills
(2-on-2 half-court wing overplay)

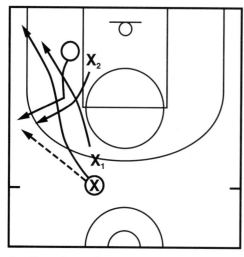

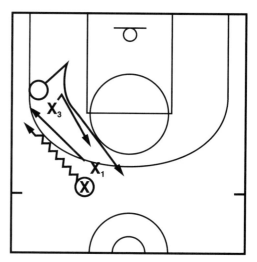

A. Guard to wing pass and guard buries in the corner. Wing can drive, pass to the corner and cut or screen on the ball. Defender on the guard must drop to the ball and ride or chuck the cutter to the corner.

B. Guard dribbles the wing out on overplay and the wing can cut away and post up or loop up to the top, opening up the side for the guard. The man defending the dribbler must deny or stop the baseline drive.

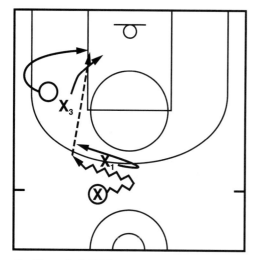

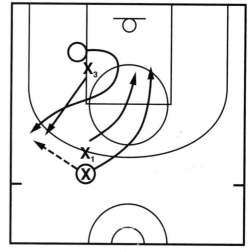

C. Guard dribbles toward the middle on the overplay of the wing and reverse dribbles, signaling the wing to go backdoor. The defender must face-guard the cutter with his back to the ball or open up and retreat to the goal.

D. Guard to wing pass as the wing curls high to the wing from the inside. The guard fakes and cuts to the goal as the defender rides him over the top, thus preventing an inside cut.

Examples of Defensive Drills
(2-on-2 half-court wing overplay)

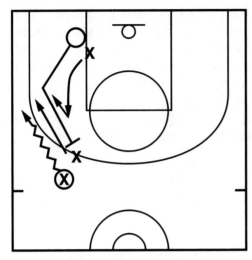

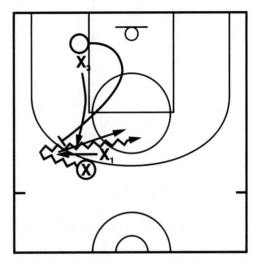

E. Defending the step up pick-and-roll.

F. Defending the step up, big for small pick-and-roll. X3 must step out and help X1 and not let the dribbler penetrate the middle. He must turn him back to his defender and the sideline or away from the basket.

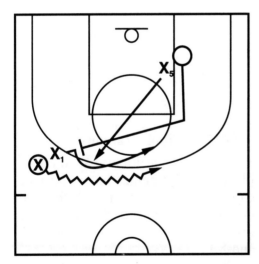

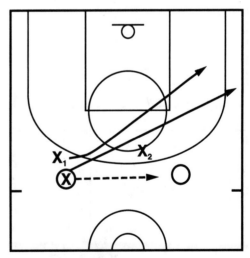

G. Defending the pick-and-roll from across the lane. X5 must stop the dribbler from turning the corner or stretching the pick-and-roll across the court.

H. Guard-to-guard pass and cut or loop. X1, the passer's defender must move in the direction of the pass as soon as the ball is in the air.

Defending Situations

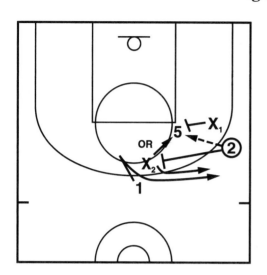

Split Post

We defend the pass to the post and guard to guard or forward to guard split by dropping level with the ball and switching and talking as the players cross. We don't let them split us. X1 and X2 must get down and even with X5's man before switching, which will eliminate the split of the switch.

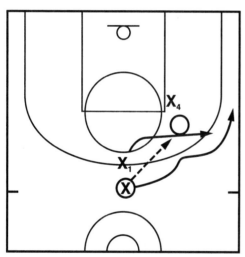

Flashing Pinch Post

We defend the flashing or pinch post by not chasing the post man and having the man on the passer drop down and in the direction of the pass to chuck or ride the cutter and deny the return pass.

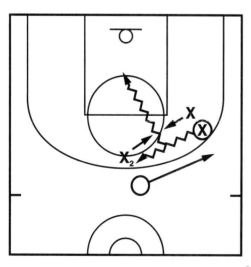

Dribble Handoff

We can switch the dribble handoff if the players come together, but we must be careful that the player with the ball doesn't fake the handoff and continue his dribble to the goal as he splits X2 and X3.

Defending Situations

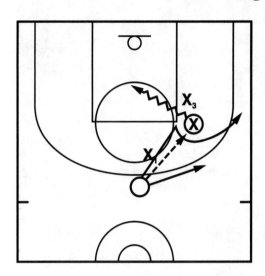

Handback

D. On the handback we have to drop down level with the ball and play this as we defend the pinch post so that the post man can't dribble-drive to the goal.

Defending the Zipper

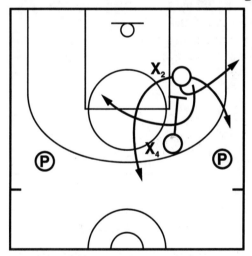

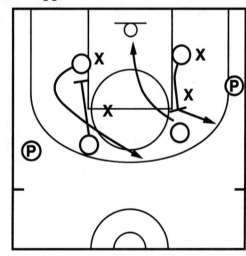

1. Downscreen
2. Fade
3. Pop out
4. Backpick

5. Screen across
6. Curl
7. Counter
8. Diagonal backpick

Photo©Frank McGrath

Splitting a double-team

Philosophy of Trapping and Double-Teaming Principles

When you trap or double-team, you may do it because you want to take the other team out of what it wants to do or because you want to change the tempo of the game. You may also double-team or trap your opponent's best player to get the ball out of his hands and make someone else try to beat you. It also may be dictated by the abilities of your players. You have to determine if you have the players capable of trapping successfully, and if you're comfortable letting your players scramble and react. You may lose a little control this way, because you can't orchestrate everything, and some coaches want to control everything. Their minds are like an engineer's. Everything has to be symmetrical. They want to know and program where each player should be during every play in the game. These coaches are reluctant to let their players scramble and react. No coach wants to let the players get completely out of control, but coaches should give players the latitude and freedom to act. Coaches can establish proper principles for double-teaming and trapping, but they should allow a little flexibility and create an atmosphere for their players to improvise and also create.

In the NBA we aren't permitted to play zone defenses, but we can double-team the ball and we are then forced to zone off of the ball or leave one player virtually alone. The best NBA defenses are man-to-man defenses with zone principles. Now you may ask, how is that possible?

The principles are that you slough off your man as far as is legally permissible and get in position to help. There are rules in the NBA that limit that help and we must adhere to them as much as possible or risk an illegal defense call and subsequent technical foul. We therefore must teach our players to anticipate and react by moving when the ball is released and in the air. At other levels, it's easier to maintain those principles, because defenses are not limited as to where the players should be and how far they must stand from the players they are defending.

Trapping enables you to take the ball out of the hands of the primary scorers and ball handlers, forcing the opposition to do something it doesn't want to do. You also trap to change tempo, have opponents make more passes than they normally do and use more of the shot clock than they are accustomed to using. Your goal is to put them into situations they aren't comfortable with and to make them put the ball in the hands of the people you want to handle it, rather than who they want to control it. Even if you aren't stealing the ball, you're still disrupting the opposition's game plan. Remember, getting your hands in the passing lanes and causing deflections can lead to turnovers, and turnovers deny your opponent a shot opportunity, give you another possession and can lead to an easy basket for your team.

Every player has to know how quick he is and how far he can go to trap. You might want to limit the distance they come to trap to six or eight feet. When you trap, you have to belly-up to the man you are trapping. You have to force him back to the player guarding him. Don't let him turn the corner. You want the trapped player to try to throw the pass over your outside shoulder, rather than permitting a penetrating pass, giving you or your teammate a chance to recover and/or intercept the pass. You want to stop your opponents from reversing the basketball. Of course, you want to move out of the trap while the ball is in the air and not wait until the ball is caught. You might want to trap the post after he has received the ball or you might want to come back and trap off of a cutter. Maybe you will decide to trap the post after one dribble or two dribbles.

Teach the defenders off the ball to read the eyes and position of the man being trapped. If he has his back turned to you, you know he won't throw it blindly over his head. Rather than anticipating where he might throw the pass, you might want to force him to throw it back out, instead of permitting a penetrating pass. If he breaks through on the dribble, you must decide if you want to release and establish position in front of him or swipe at the ball from behind. Decide if you want to double the baseline drive and then decide if you want to beat the driver to a spot or if you want to steal the ball from behind. If you're fronting the post and they drive on the baseline, do you leave the post and jump out on the ball? Who then covers the post? You must decide and then teach and practice how you want your players to react and rotate in each instance.

Double-Teaming and Trapping Rules

1. When do you trap? On the pass, on the dribble, from behind when their back is turned.

2. If you use traps you must stop the inside cut. Don't let weak side offensive players flash cut to the ball as outlets.

3. When trapping wings, take away the outlet pass.

4. When trapping, leave the farthest man away from the ball free.

5. Recognize and practice the proper weak side rotation.

6. The three men off the ball should cover the sideline, middle and basket in your full court press trapping defense. Make your opponent throw the ball back outside and don't permit a penetrating pass out of a trap.

7. Trap and move when the pass is in the air, not when the ball has been caught. MOVE ON THE PASS, NOT ON THE CATCH!

8. Trap on the first dribble, second dribble, or fake going to double the ball.

9. Create a signal for when you double from in front of the dribbler and another for when you double him from behind.

10. If you force the pass backward, zone up and continue to trap.

11. If you force the pass forward, match up and play man-to-man.

12. Decide if you are going to trap once and retreat to man-to-man or again trap when they reach midcourt.

13. Stay in the double team until the pass is made. Double hard when the ball is picked up by the trapped player. Don't leave until the pass is released and in the air.

14. Players off the ball should read the trapped player's eyes. Try to anticipate where he will throw the ball.

15. Make the trapped player throw the ball over your outside shoulder. Trap and seal the middle.

16. Belly-up and seal on double teams. Take away the baseline and turn the trapped player to the double team. Don't let them split the trap and pass through it.

17. When to trap? Know how fast you are and how many steps you need to trap. Perhaps establish a rule that limits your trapping distance to six or eight feet, etc.

18. Trap from behind when the man turns his back to the defense.

19. Trap to cause the player to pass the ball immediately upon receiving a pass before he can think about making an offensive move.

20. The best places to double team and trap are near the sidelines, baseline, the corners and the midcourt line.

21. Decide if you want to trap from either the passer, from the top, weak side, off of the other big man or coming back from the cutter once you are below the post man with the ball. Vary your traps. Don't permit the offense to become comfortable.

22. When trapping out on the court, trap from in front, when you are level with the ball and also from behind if the offensive man you are guarding is trailing the play.

23. Once committed to trapping, continue to come hard. Don't stop or hesitate and get caught in no-man's land.

24. Establish a signal to alert your players that your team is trapping and from where you are going to trap.

25. Off the ball defenders should be alert to pick up offensive fouls.

26. Stay attached to the shooters. Lock in and don't permit them to get free. MARRY THEM.

27. Trap the dribbler with your 4 or 5 if their man trails the ball.

28. Think about trapping the wing with the ball early on isolation plays or before the pick or screen can be set.

29. Immediately rotate back to the goal once the pass is made out of the trap, especially if the trapped player is not your man. Obstruct the passing and driving lanes.

30. Decide if rotating players are to go toward the goal and get the free man in the direction of the help or rush back to the originally assigned player they were defending.

31. Practice how to trap. Demonstrate and drill.

32. The three weak side men not involved in the half-court trap must zone up and cover the weak side, middle and basket, perhaps leaving the offensive man farthest away from the ball free. Pressure the ball or passer.

33. When trapping wings we must front the low post and deny the nearest outlets.

Teaching how and when to trap

Set up situations on the floor. Break down every situation in every area of the court. You should create and explain your rules for defending each situation. You can cover full court, half court, sideline or post. Set up drills, three-on-three or four-on-four, where you show which player is in the best position to help on the trap and how the other defensive players should react to and read the trap. Interchange the players so everyone knows how to react to any situation anywhere on the court and each is aware of how to trap and rotate from a given area. Emphasize the players not involved in the trap always cover the near sideline, middle and basket in an effort to cover the most obvious and dangerous outlets.

Use the half-court Shell Drill to go over each situation. Practice it repeatedly. Explain each situation. You might have different rules for your basic defense than you have for your trapping defense and these have to be ingrained and taught.

Drill for Trapping the Dribbler

A. A great drill to teach trapping the dribbler is to put two defenders against one offensive man in the backcourt for 10 seconds. Emphasize leveling with the ball and trapping the ball handler forcing him to pick up his dribble and/or relinquish the ball.

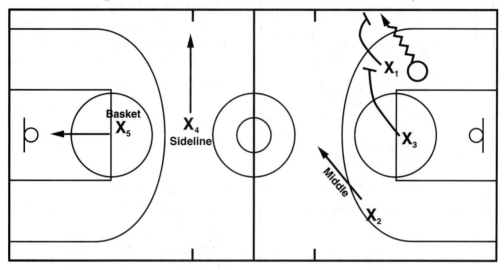

B. The same drill can be run in the half court. Two defenders force the point guard to the sideline to trap and double him.

Rules:

1. The last defender over half court traps the ball and forces it sideline.

2. We use our same man-to-man/zone/man-to-man principles.

3. On the near sideline we over play in man-to-man denial, forcing the receiver back door.

4. The middle man is man-to-man, trying to smother and deny the outlet.

5. The basket man zones up and covers the basket.

Three-quarter court defense:

If the man dribbles to the middle, our middle man traps from in front.

If the man dribbles sideline we trap from behind and our other players, zone level with the ball and rotate back to take away the passing lanes.

Defensive Pick-and-Roll Drills

(A) (Defending the pick-and-roll)

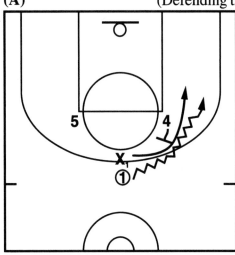

Mullaney Drill

A. We begin with a dribbler defended (1-on-1) and two post men undefended who talk as defensive players and catch passes, but also set screens and step out as offensive players.

(B)

2. We teach the defender to make himself thinner as he steps up and to the outside of the dribbler and fights over the screen. We run this drill from the center field, corner and wing positions.

(C)

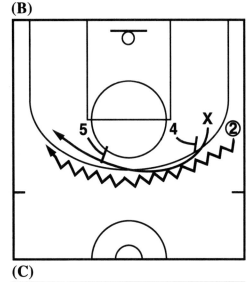

(C) We then add two defensive post men and continue the drill. We will practice these defensive maneuvers:

1. Sideline the pick-and-roll
2. Jump and trap the pick-and-roll
3. Help and hedge or show to slow penetration as the guard fights over the screen
4. Jump the dribbler with the post man before the pick can be set
5. Squeeze or hug the screener and going under to avoid the pick and stop the dribbler from turning the corner
6. Sliding through the defender on the screener and the screener

Pick-and-Roll Defense

Objective: Don't let them penetrate and turn the corner. You must slow them up and turn them back or out on the perimeter.

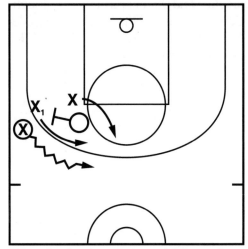

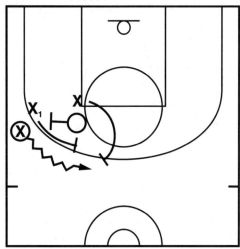

Wing Defender: Force middle and get over; big man hard show hedge and/or trap.

Wing Defender: Force middle; go through and inside the screener's defender.

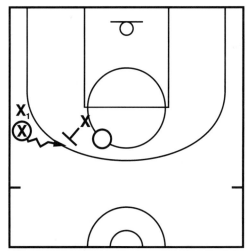

Wing Defender: Force middle and big man trap before screen can be set.

Wing: Big man pick or squeeze the screener. Wing Defender: Go behind defensive big man.

We practice these same pick-and-roll defenses from the middle of the court and in the corners. We want our big men to stay attached to the screeners. Our keys or signals are one of the following: a) colors; b) terms; c) letters; d) numbers.

Pick-and-Roll Defense

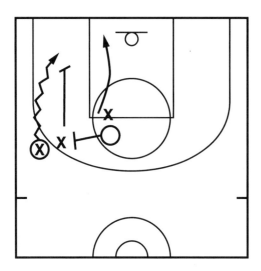

Wing: Ball defender forces the dribbler sideline and screener's defender sloughs down and toward the baseline and sideline to help the defender on the ball. He could trap if feasible.

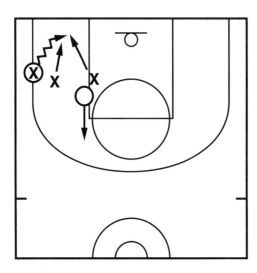

Corner: Force sideline; trap and double baseline drive; should be easier to zone on the weak side. Beware of offensive post man stepping up the lane to establish position to break the pressure.

Example of Defensive Drills
(2-on-2 half-court wing overplay)

A. Guard to wing pass and guard buries in the corner. Wing can drive, pass to the corner and cut or screen on the ball. Defender on the guard must drop to the ball and ride or chuck the cutter to the corner.

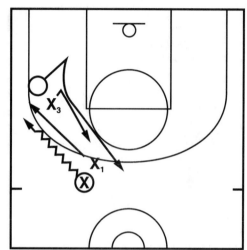

B. Guard dribbles the wing out on overplay and the wing can cut away and post up or loop up to the top, opening up the side for the guard. The man defending the dribbler must deny or stop the baseline drive.

C. Guard dribbles towards the middle on the overplay of the wing and reverse dribbles, signaling the wing to go backdoor. The defender must face the guard cutter with his back to the ball or open up and retreat to the goal.

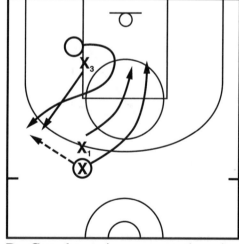

D. Guard to wing pass as the wing curls high to the wing from the inside. The guard fakes and cuts to the goal as the defender rides him over the top, thus preventing an inside cut.

Example of Defensive Drills
(2-on-2 half-court wing overplay)

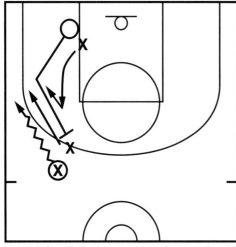

E. Defending the step up pick-and-roll.

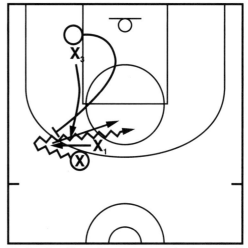

F. Defending the step up, big for small pick-and-roll.

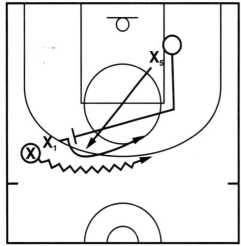

G. Defending the pick-and-roll from across the lane.

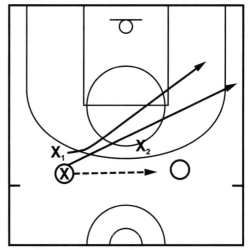

H. Guard-to-guard pass and cut or loop. The passer's defender must move in the direction of the pass.

Defending the pick-and-roll

Each coach has to decide how he wants his team to play the middle pick-and-roll, the wing pick-and-roll and the step-up pick-and-roll. You have to decide if you are to double it or show hard and fight over it. When we show hard, we step out to slow the dribbler and to help the guard recover. You must decide when to squeeze it, slide through, go over the top, force it sideline or trap it before they even have a chance to set the pick? Do you want to teach one or two ways to defend the pick-and-roll or a number of ways to stop it? It's the coach's call, but you must be flexible and prepared to adjust according to your opponent and the ability of your players.

Pick-and-Roll Rules

1. Double pick-and-rolls, when, where side/top/corner.

2. Decide who picks up the roll man after the dribbler has penetrated and the man rolls to the goal and/or slides to the corner or steps back. Where does the screener's defender then go?

3. On the 1-3 or 1-2, wing or middle step back or post up, do we switch, slide, stay attached, squeeze the help and recover?

4. On the 1-4, 1-5 side pick-and-roll, do we double or come early to prevent the pick-and-roll by not letting them set the pick?

5. Squeeze the high pick-and-roll above the three-point line if the dribbler is not a good shooter.

6. Don't let the dribbler turn the corner. Both defenders are responsible for stopping his penetration.

7. You can use colors (red, green, blue, white) to signal which method you will use to defend pick-and-rolls. Many teams use letters or key words as signals.

8. You can switch big men on pick the picker back picks on the pick-and-roll.

9. You might want to disguise your tactic by yelling "switch," but still helping and recovering on the pick-and-roll.

■ You also have to determine how to play the loop, instead of the pick-and-roll. What do you do if they pick the picker on the pick-and-roll? Do you switch this backpick even if it then creates a mismatch? Your decision should be determined by the abilities of the screener.

Offensive Principles

Establish, explain and then teach your offensive philosophy. Some coaches believe in having multiple offenses or options, and we believe this is probably a fine idea. They want their players to be versatile. They don't limit their players, but they make sure each knows his individual strengths and limitations as well as that of his teammates'. We also want to run, because we want to create easy baskets. We want a great deal of ball and player movement to move the defense. Our players must be intelligent and be able to react to any situation. Coaches should feel confident that they have prepared their players for any eventuality. We like to play baseline-to-baseline, 94 feet of offense and we want to score off our defense. We want our players to always know the score and time. They must be able to penetrate and go inside-out, but we want to get the ball inside first. We constantly try to have the defense adjust to us. We don't want to settle for outside jumpers before we move the defense, unless it's an opportunity shot and the backboard is covered. We make our opponents cover the whole floor so they'll have a tough time keeping up with us the whole game. We want to pass, cut, move, screen and reverse the ball. We want every player to be aware of where the other nine players are. They should always keep an eye on the man who passed the ball or the offensive man in front of them, because most times he tells you what's happening by his individual movement. Players should understand how to play cat-and-mouse to get free and take advantage of defensive lapses. They must learn to close the distance between themselves and their defenders. They must be able to change direction and change speed. They must know how to use every offensive weapon available, whether they be cross screens, lobs, backdoor moves, isolations and/or diagonal cuts. Remember, everything we learn to execute offensively ultimately will also make us a better defensive team, because we'll have learned how to defend every conceivable offensive option.

We believe teaching multiple offense really makes your players more versatile and effective both offensively and defensively.

Force the break, but not the bad shot.

Offensive rules we try to incorporate in our system

1. Have your point man call out and signal your plays. Encourage another player to repeat his call or signal so that every player is aware of what you are running in case the first call or signal was missed or arena noise has drowned out the signal.

2. Instill in your players the fact that good offensive basketball includes taking the ball inside and from one side to the other by reversing the ball in order to move the defense.

3. Watch the man who passed the ball. What he does next will tell you what the offensive team is trying to do or possibly what play it is trying to run. Some coaches say watch what the offensive player in front of the ball does to dictate what your next move should be.

4. If there is a missed shot on your defensive end, recover the ball, push it ahead and hit the open man for an easy score.

5. (a) If the point pushes the ball in transition or on the fast break and he sees the numbers advantage is more than two, he should pass and cut. (b) If numbers are less than two, he should drive the wing out and penetrate and look for a shot.

6. Make a commitment as to when you are going to run: after makes, misses or both.

7. Run plays at your opponents' best offensive threats. Force them to play defense and not concentrate solely on offense.

8. On a baseline drive, teach your big men to step up the lane to be in a scoring area if the defense rotates or traps the dribbler.

9. The passer and receiver should establish eye contact as a means of communication to establish passing lanes.

10. Weakside offensive men must dive to the goal, up the gut if their defenders double or trap. Try to get inside the defender to receive a pass or be in position to grab a rebound.

11. When facing pressure on the point in the backcourt, big men must know to blind screen the defender in the backcourt pressuring the point or to serve as an outlet for the give-and-go pass.

12. When scissoring or splitting high and low or pinch post, the passer usually cuts and screens first and then the other offensive player cuts off his back.

13. To "ice" or isolate a superior one-on-one player, you can downscreen and cross, curl and screen, pop and curl from the stack to step out or you can pass to the man on the wing and cut away.

14. Wings must first run for layups on the break, then they can look to screen across or pop back out.

15. On crossing action in transition, fast-break or half-court offense, the weakside cutter can curl the screener, cross to the corner, set a UCLA upblock for the high post man, set a diagonal screen for the trailer or post up if the screener vacates the area.

16. Make simple passes, not always home run or scoring passes.

17. Try to work on making two-hand over-the-head passes to set up the backdoor, to fake and to establish eye contact with the man you are trying to pass to.

18. When making the post pass, throw to a target away from the defender and throw good crisp passes by the defender's ear or over his head. Also teach your players how to utilize the hard bounce pass as a means of feeding the post.

19. Always pass to the open man.

20. Four or five passes will move the defense, open up offensive opportunities and help deter opponents' fast breaks.

21. Teach your team to recognize mismatches and encourage them to take advantage of all of these mismatches.

22. Teach players without the ball to cut backdoor or dive to the goal if their defender turns his back or goes to help double-team.

23. Take the ball 94 feet and then inside-out and over if you don't have a fast break. Make the defense cover the entire court.

24. Always look to go inside first, rather than begin shooting from the outside.

25. Learn to break pressure and denial with the backdoor, weakside flash or pinch post entry.

26. After making a layup off a breakaway or making a steal, immediately pressure and "multiply" to get another basket right away.

27. Don't permit your opponents to force your point guard to the sideline. Teach him to split the sideline and midcourt, keep his dribble alive and teach your other players to loop to split the defenders and open up the court for the dribbler.

28. If the point or wing dribbles at the high post being overplayed, he must immediately recognize this and dive to the goal.

29. The dribble is designed to penetrate, cover distance, advance the ball and help you get out of trouble.

30. Read the defense and make and take different paths on cuts which forces the defense to make decisions and react to you.

31. Drive and penetrate the defense to go to the goal or to create penetrate-and-pitch opportunities.

32. Quick shots without rebounding coverage will start your opponents' fast breaks.

33. Work your man to get free on the wing. Fake and freeze him, pop, curl, step over his outside foot or go up the lane and widen out.

34. Weakside players must screen, move, fake and close the distance on their defenders to keep them occupied and denying them the opportunity to help.

35. Don't drive to the corners and pick up your dribble. This invites the defense to trap you by using the sideline and baseline as defenders.

36. When overplayed, a backdoor cut or loop is automatic if the ball is being dribbled toward you.

37. If the opponents score three baskets in a row, we should concentrate on calling a play and getting a sure basket. Get organized and drive the ball.

38. You can establish a rule that after every three passes the ball must go into the post. Don't just throw perimeter passes.

39. If the defense chases over the top of scissors when we cross on the baseline, the screeners should step up and into the lane looking to receive a pass.

40. Be especially aware of not committing turnovers after steals or rebounds, thus giving the ball back to your opponents.

41. Have sets where small players pick big players, causing defenses to make decisions by creating mismatch opportunities.

42. Teach your big players to circle behind the defense on the baseline and attack from behind with the ball in the opposite corner.

43. Versus defensive switching on the double stack cross we can throw back and post our big men or step one of the crossing players up into the lane.

44. Bend your knees when setting the screen for the pick-and-roll and pivot with the force of the blow. Seal the defender on your back.

45. Establish a rule stating when a man passes to the post he has to cut to the goal and look for a return pass or screen away and head hunt.

46. If you pass and cut, the next offensive man must replace you.

47. If we change sides with the ball, look for someone to screen.

48. If you set a backscreen, don't always step back. Sometimes step out to the wing to create an easier passing lane and open up the court.

49. Setting a backpick for a teammate is one of the best ways to create a scoring opportunity for yourself.

All players, but especially point guards, should keep their heads up when dribbling so they can see the goal and the other nine players.

Photo©Frank McGrath

The classic jump shot

Building
an Offense

Qualities of a good offense

When constructing an offense, a coach should consider whether or not it includes the following things:

- Provides the team with an opportunity to penetrate to the goal to get an easy or open shot.

- Has players spaced 15-20 feet apart on the court, permitting any player with the ball the ability to throw a pass to any of the other four offensive players and that each of these players should also be in scoring position.

- Enables movement of the players and ball toward the purpose of obtaining a good scoring opportunity.

- Provides advantageous offensive rebounding position and optimum defensive balance on all shots.

- Incorporates a five-man concept providing offensive opportunities for each player. It utilizes the individual talents of each player and again enables him to pass to any of his four teammates.

- Provides all players the opportunity to read the defense and gives them the ability to effectively counter defensive pressure and adjustments.

113

Spacing Drill

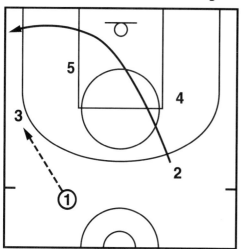

Players spaced above the three-point line make the entry passes higher on the court, which takes away pressure defense or makes the defense cover a much greater area. This establishes much clearer passing and penetrating lanes.

Go the length of the court

Design drills that require the team to go the length of the court. Whether they are one-on-one or five-on-five drills, design them to go the length of the floor. Build the offense methodically by going two-on-none, three-on-none, four-on-none and five-on-none. Demonstrate and show each player each thing you want him to do. There are only a limited number of options for every player on a given play, no matter who the player might be.

■ He can shoot.

■ He can dribble.

■ He can pass and cut.

■ He can pass and screen away.

■ He can pass and cut through to either corner.

■ He can pass and get the ball back.

■ He can pass and screen the man with the ball.

■ Or he can pass and replace himself. (We won't permit our players to stand still on offense. They have to move without the ball.)

Your players should understand to key their eyes on the ball offensively. Watch the man who passes the ball. Invariably by his actions or movement, he'll let you know what the team is trying to do. Keeping your eye on the ball offensively is just as important as keeping your eye on the ball defensively. By watching the offensive man in front of the player with the ball we can get the same result.

We begin teaching all of these options in dummy offensive sets without a defense. First we go two-on-none. Then three-on-none. One player passes and the other players execute all of the available options. Before they know it, they've covered every possibility. If you do this every day or every other day, it will become spontaneous. You also must emphasize that your players should always

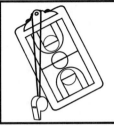

Make sure you run your offense to both sides of the floor. Don't become a one-sided team that is easier to defend.

establish eye contact with each other. This reinforces why seeing the ball on offense is important. Eye contact is often the most effective way of communicating on the court and leads to easy baskets.

Out-of-bounds plays

An area that a lot of coaches overlook and don't work on enough is out-of-bounds plays. Think about how many times during a game the ball is put into play from out of bounds:

- After every basket.
- Every timeout.
- Quarter or halftime breaks.
- Every violation.
- Every time the ball is knocked out of bounds.
- Every foul until a team is shooting the bonus.
- Every held ball (at some levels of play).
- Every time an official has a question about the clock or score.
- After technical fouls.

Add these up. In a pro game, that can mean as many as 100 plays on offense and 100 plays on defense. Too many times coaches use an out-of-bounds play to just get the ball in play. They forget about scoring quickly by taking advantage of defensive lapses. Many coaches use the same player to throw the inbounds pass every time. Some coaches never contest an inbounds pass in the backcourt. Your players must recognize the difference between an out-of-bounds play from the end line (after a basket), sideline out of bounds in the backcourt or frontcourt, or out of bounds under your own basket. You should have a strategy both offensively and defensively for every situation and not be satisfied with just getting the ball inbounds. Teach the players how to inbound, where to stand and to count to themselves to avoid a five-second violation. Also take advantage of your inbounds passer if he is a superior offensive player by getting him the ball after he inbounds it.

You might want to use number options for specific cuts such as "3" for screen across the lane or "4" to signal a backpick.

Types of
Offensive
Sets

You can use one or several types of offensive sets. Most offenses can be run from more than one set. There are one-guard fronts, two-guard fronts, unbalanced sets, box sets, and single and double stacks. There are sets you use when you are going for the last shot in the quarter or last shot in the game. There are different sets for sideline out-of-bounds plays and baseline out-of-bounds plays. There are sets for special plays that you might only use once a game and sets you might automatically go into when there's a short amount of time left on the shot clock or when you want a two-for-one opportunity. It is the coach's responsibility to utilize sets that take advantage of and maximize rather than limit his players' talents and abilities. At times this is a trial and error process that you work on in your daily practices and meetings. Sometimes it is a good idea to ask the players what offensive tactic they can use most efficiently to maximize their own individual offensive skills. If it's feasible, you may want to incorporate some of these in your offense.

Offensive Cuts
(2-on-2 or 3-on-3)

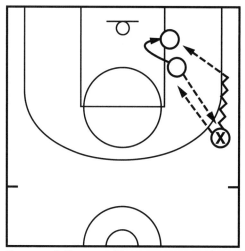

Post and Repost. Repost to get closer to the goal by throwing the ball out to gain better position.

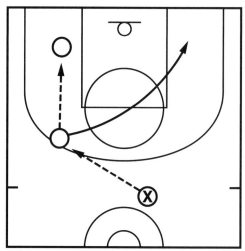

Direct or Drop to isolate a man on the low post.

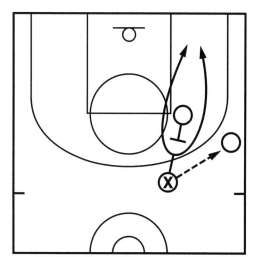

UCLA Cut. The cutter uses the screen from the high post to cut either way to the goal.

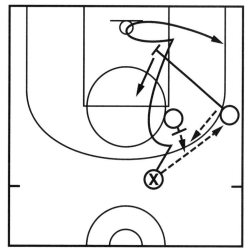

UCLA Cut and Pin Down. Take your defender into the paint and wait for the wing to screen your defender.

Offensive Cuts
(2-on-2 or 3-on-3)

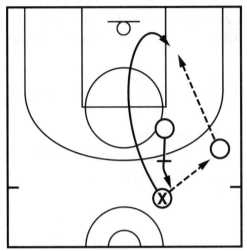

UCLA Cut and Post-up.

UCLA cut or cut away and pick-and-roll. The post comes to the wing for the pick-and-roll following the guard's UCLA cut.

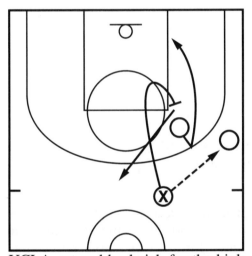

UCLA cut and backpick for the high post.

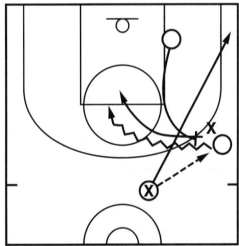

Point to wing, bury and step up wing pick-and-roll.

Last Shot in the Quarter (LSQ) or Last Shot in the Game (LSG)

Why last-second plays should be practiced.

A. It provides an opportunity to test your plays against all types of defenses.

B. Instead of diagramming a new play during a timeout, you have more time to review what you want your team to do after running the play. You can set the options, the defensive assignments, etc.

C. It's also important to remind all the players not to watch and hope the shot goes in or doesn't go in. The most important thing is to box out or go to the goal to rebound a miss or put the ball back in the basket.

D. A prepared team is usually more confident in what it is doing.

E. It gives you an opportunity to also practice defending last-shot situations.

Rebounding and Transition, Offense and Defense
(4-on-4 or 5-on-5)

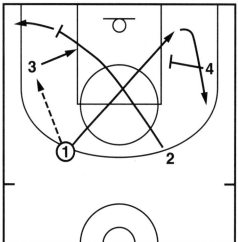

A. Movement, three or four passes, shot, box out, fast break.

B. Give up an offensive rebound, you stay on defense one more time.

C. Transition retreat into a certain defense.

Defending Game Situations
(3-on-3, half court)

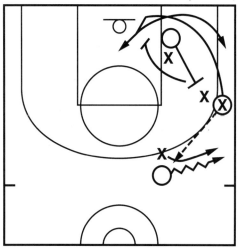

Backpick for the wing after passing to the top and then repick on pindown action for the wing who breaks to the corner or steps up into the lane.

Defending Game Situations
(3-on-3, half court)

Staggered double baseline screen for the shooter.

Defending the flex cut and low post stepping in after the cut is made.

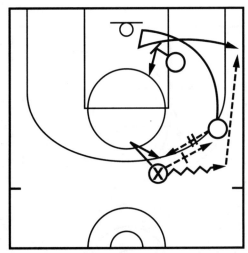

Guard-to-wing pass and return pass to point and then wing cuts into the lane to receive a screen from the low post man. We must also defend the next pass from wing to post.

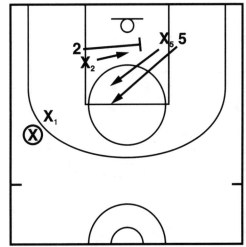

Small player screening a big player across the lane. It is the responsibility of X5 to ride the man up the lane. If 5 cuts baseline, X2 must bump and slow him until X5 arrives.

Defending 4-on-4
(Half court)

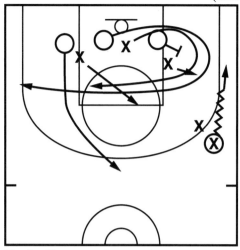

Curl off post and post up.

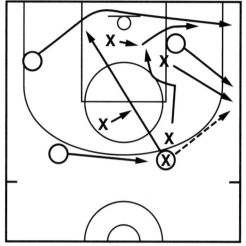

Pass to wing and cut away to the goal as weakside forward clears to the strong side.

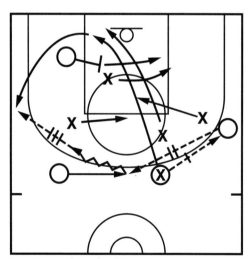

Pass to wing and cut away, receive a screen for ball reversal from the replacing guard.

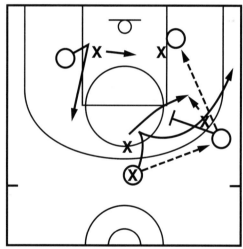

Pass to wing, wing to post and wing and guard split weak side. Post lifts to take away weakside help.

Defending 4-on-4
(Half court)

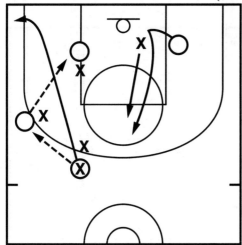

Guard-to-wing pass, guard buries, wing-to-post pass as weakside forward comes up the lane for lock-and-lob in case the low post is fronted. We must pressure the passers on post ups to help the low-post defenders guard their opponents.

Guard dribbles to the wing, screen across for post up and pick-the-picker action from the high post. We may want to decide to switch X2 and X3 in certain situations.

Defending double screens on a loop cut from the corner to the top.

Dribble penetration to hit guard coming off either low post man. Some teams chase O2 coming off of the screen on the strong side; others shoot the gap and go over the top.

We also work at defending staggered screens, the single double baseline stack and any other maneuvers we may face. We design and set up drills to enable us to practice game situations.

123

Options for an Offensive Player After Passing the Ball

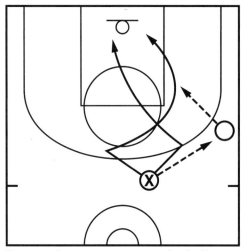

Pass and cut —cutter see the ball.
  a. Step to the ball and cut away
  b. Step away from the ball and cut to the ball through the lane (give-and-go)

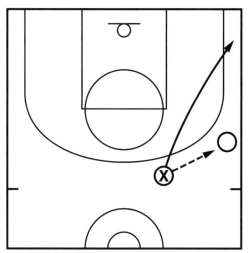

Pass and bury — wing can pass and/or drive.

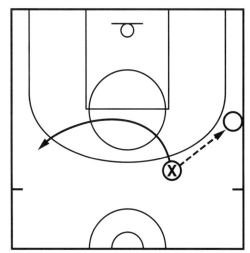

Pass and shallow cut away (almost a loop maneuver) The wing is now isolated on his defender.

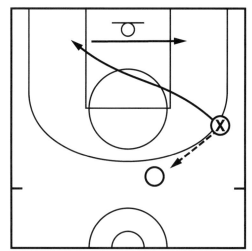

Wing to point pass and cut and come back to post up as the guard dribbles to the wing to create a pass into the lane.

In the above situations the man with the ball can also dribble the other man out.

Options for an Offensive Player After Passing the Ball

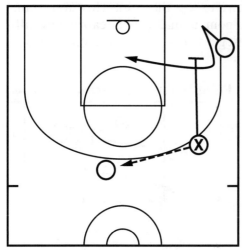

Pass and screen away and then pop back.

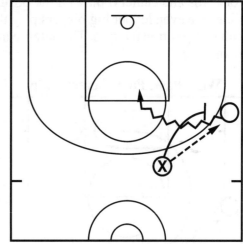

Pass and screen the ball.

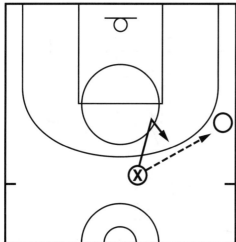
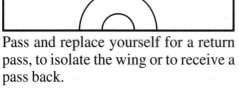

Pass and replace yourself for a return pass, to isolate the wing or to receive a pass back.

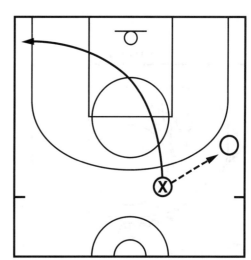

Pass and bury away — isolate the wing.

When passing and cutting, it is important that the cutting player always looks for the return pass. He must see the ball so the threat of a return pass keeps the defense from cheating and helping off the ball. He should also be aware of the screening for another man or two as he cuts.

Half- or Full-Court Three-Man Game

We have three lines off the court and keep rotating groups. Our point men, shooting guards and small forwards play all the positions and our big men (power forwards and centers) play all the positions, except the point. However, sometimes we even let our big players play the point to make them realize how difficult that position really is. The defense must get at least one stop before it changes to offense.

Wing Pass, Point Screens Big

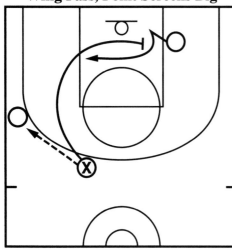

Point Dribble, Big Screens Across

Turnout

Turnout, Curl, Post Up

Half- or Full-Court Three-Man Game

Wing Pass, Screen Across for Pick-and-Roll

Wing Pass with Backpick for Point

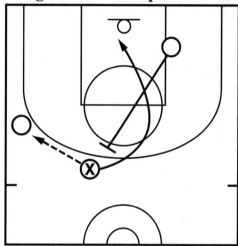

Dribble Out Wing, Loop, Post-Up

Direct Post-Up, Elbow Pass and Cut

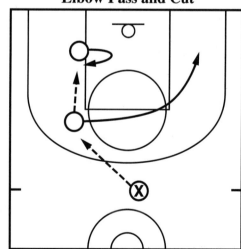

This is only a sampling of some of the options we set up. We do similar drilling 4-on-4 to also work on our execution, timing and spacing.

Fast-Break

Principles

Develop a philosophy and explain to your players what you feel are the advantages of the fast break and running north to south, rather than east to west.

Teams generally like to fast break because it creates easy baskets. Your team will shoot a much higher percentage shooting layups than it will jump shots. You want to create easy scoring opportunities where you have a one- or two-man advantage. But you must teach your players when you want them to fast break. Decide whether you want to run after makes, after misses or all the time. Do you break using the dribble or long passes? Do you run a sideline or middle break? Your team must also know when you prefer it didn't fast break. The players have to be aware of the score, time and tempo of the game. They need to understand how that affects their decision making. When you break, you should want to run the length of the court, all 94 feet. You want to run and move the ball in, out and over, from every direction. You might spot up in the corners or cross your wings underneath. If you don't get a quick layup, you might want to swing the ball out and get into a quick, early or secondary offense. Perhaps you want to look for a man diving into the lane and posting up. You might still get a mismatch or an easy jumper, because it's tough for the defense to pick up their men if they've been chasing other players down the court. Decide how and where you want your first big man to go. Do you want him to run to the middle of the court directly to the goal or to the ballside block, etc? Some coaches prefer big men to run out wide and then to the ballside block.

Set up and regularly practice quick scoring opportunities with no timeouts, a few seconds on the shot or game clock and other need situations when teaching the break after a rebound, from an out-of-bounds situation, off of a steal or after a basket.

Prepare, practice, execute! Simulate game conditions in your practices.

You need to determine if you always want a layup or if you will be satisfied with a spot-up jumper from the corner or 15 feet as long as the board is covered. Do you want to run on free throws made or missed? If your opponents are pressing you, do you want to still look for the break, forcing them to defend full court, or do you want to get across the time line and immediately get into your secondary offense? These are all coaching decisions you must make and then they should be ingrained in the minds of all your players. You might want to emphasize always "forcing the break, but not the bad shot!"

If you want to fast break, you have to teach the players who you want inbounding the ball and who you want receiving the ball. Explain whether you prefer advancing the ball up the court on the dribble or with quick and long passes. Do you want your players to leak out on every long shot by your opponent or to wait until your team gains possession of the ball? Do you favor a sideline or middle break or a combination of both?

Fast breaks put a lot of pressure on the defenses. They are forced to pick up men in unfamiliar areas in transition and this creates mismatches and indecision.

It is the individual coach's decision whether or not to establish a rule that states you can only run off of misses. You should want to teach your players to push the ball and look for the break when you have numbers and/or players free or running down court. They have to recognize and capitalize on opportunities for easy baskets.

Things to remember about fast breaks

1. Have your ball handlers protect, push and keep their dribble in front of them so the ball can't be swiped and stolen from behind.

2. Look to pass the ball ahead, not behind.

3. The free man ahead of you should always receive the ball.

4. Have your wings run for layups and if the layup or pass isn't there, make them cross underneath or quickly widen out and pop to the corners.

5. When you cross underneath, the wing crossing on the ball side should always be the screener to avoid collisions.

6. When the wings cross with the ball in the middle, designate a side for a man to go high (man or ball side) to avoid collisions.

7. Teams that only run on misses are usually vulnerable because they don't expect opponents to run on makes.

8. Outlet long — above the free-throw line. It gets the ball down the floor quicker and also spreads the defense and makes it more difficult for the man playing the inbound pass to trap the first pass.

9. You may want the nearest big man or designated passer to get to the ball and inbound it quickly before the defense has time to establish or set up its defense or you may want to set up your press offense before passing the ball.

10. A dribbler can drive from the sideline to the middle or across the court and change sides to go against the grain and flow of retreating defenses causing them to make hurried decisions.

11. A wing crossing on the baseline can curl, post, go to the strongside corner, upblock the high post in UCLA action, diagonally upblock the trailer or post up if the screener vacates the area.

12. You can start your offense or fast break off of your pressure defense.

13. Don't inbound the ball under the backboard. It cuts down your passing angles and your pass might hit the backboard and go out of bounds causing you to lose the ball.

14. It is not a bad idea to inbound from the left side as you face the court, because most defenses expect you to go to your right to inbound. That's where they expect you to pass and where they practice springing their trap.

15. Wings and big men running lanes must run wide to spread the defense.

16. Set screens on interchanges outside the three-point line. Head hunt defenders and create good spacing.

17. The middle man on the break should step toward the elbow in the direction of the pass to make room for the trailer cutting to the basket and to provide an outlet in case the man receiving the ball doesn't have an open shot.

18. Outlets should be on either side when beginning the fast break. Don't limit beginning your fast break to only one side of the court.

19. A good tactic is to have your first big man run the middle of the floor in front of the ball to get post position in the middle of the lane.

Teaching Fast-Break Organization

Coaches need to break down the fast break into all its possible components when explaining it to their players. Decide if it works best to have your team advance the ball with the dribble or with quick passes. Coaches who use the long pass figure that it is faster and easier to cover distance with the pass. Sometimes it can also be more dangerous. You must practice those passes on a daily basis. This will give you an opportunity to adjust to different defensive tactics. You have to decide if you want the ball in the middle or if you want a sideline break. Maybe you want to vary and combine the two. Your goal should be to create good opportunity shots and how you best achieve that is what is most important.

When you practice, go two-on-none, three-on-none, four-on-none and five-on-none until everyone is comfortable with what he is doing and where he should be on the break. What does the first big man do? (Does he go straight down the middle to the post or to the ballside block?) What does the trailer do? Does he go wide, go to the basket, set a screen or be in center field in a position to swing or reverse the basketball?

Next set up situations: Run the fast break off a turnover in front court, from midcourt or three-quarter court; fast break after made or missed free throws, run after capturing a long rebound, and even practice fast breaking from an out-of-bounds situation on the side, under the basket or immediately following a time out. You fast break whenever you can create an easy scoring opportunity and it enables you to always try to put and maintain pressure on the defense.

Position and place your players so they know where to throw and where to receive the outlet pass. What should the player do when he receives the outlet pass? Should he immediately turn and dribble or do you first want him to turn and look up court to better see the defense to make a pass to advance the ball?

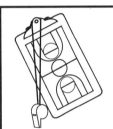

Always pass ahead to the free or open man on the fast break. Get him the ball.

Points to remember when fast breaking off a free throw

1. After a basket you can pass behind the baseline to a man who has stepped out of bounds which will break ball pressure and provide better passing lanes.

2. After a basket the inbounder can run the baseline.

3. Dive men to the board from above the circle to rebound once the shot is released.

4. "X." Have the rebounders from the middle positions on the lane cross and screen for each other and look for offensive rebounds should the shooter miss the free throw.

5. Go around the rebounder from the middle position and get to the inside to try to rebound offensively.

6. Miss purposely (down two or three points) with little time on the clock. Practice this tactic and where the ball will bounce so you can retrieve it and quickly score.

7. Box out the shooter. Which man has this responsibility? The nearest man on the lane or a defender positioned outside the free-throw circle?

8. Pinch or seal the strongest rebounder.

9. Spread the court 94 feet. Space out your players to stretch the defense. Try to cover the 94 feet with quick passes, a maximum of one or two.

10. You should be able to go from one end of the court to the other and get a good shot and score in five seconds or less.

11. You must prove to your players how long five seconds really is when you have no timeouts left.

12. Set a blind screen for the inbounds passer, enabling him to receive the next pass or to run full speed to the goal, looking for a surprise scoring pass or to open up the court for the next option.

Fast Break Drills

A. Rebound and outlet
B. Three-line drills
C. Three-line weave
D. 2-minute drill
E. Inside-out
F. Four-out with a trailer
G. Five-out

H. Three-line jump shot
I. Four-line up and out
J. 3-on-2, 2-on-1
K. 4-on-3, 3-on-2
L. Same with a defender trailing (4-on-4, 3-on-3)
M. Off a free throw (make or miss)
N. Last-second plays

Fast Break Drill
(Two-man game options)

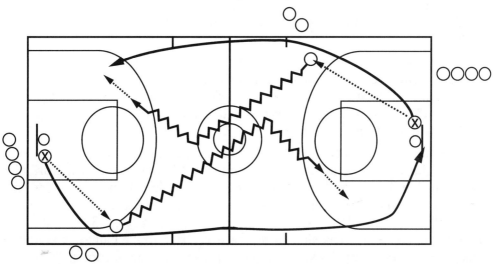

Two balls at the same time, one at each basket. Rebound and pass to the outlet man, follow the pass and run various 2-man play options. Examples of some options:

1. Give-and-go
2. Pass, return pass and cut
3. Fake and drive
4. Reverse dribble and backdoor
5. Dribble wing out to the post up
6. Pass and pick the point of the ball for the pick-and-roll
7. Dribble out to loop
8. Pass and bury
9. Pass for a wing jump shot
10. Penetrate and pitch to a shooter

133

Fast-Break Organization
(Warm-up drill — early in practice)

Three lines of players on one baseline who pass and go full court with the ball and make the basket as we run for a layup on the other end.

Diagram A: We begin with the ball in one of the wing lines (with an equal number of players, each group of three has a basketball on the same wing) and the wing and middle man pass back and forth until crossing midcourt with the ball in the possession of the middle man. The middle man then dribbles across and ahead, above the free throw circle and even with the opposite elbow area to pass to the opposite wing running wide and breaking his cut for a layup at a little above the foul line extended. The coach determines if the scoring pass is to be a chest or bounce pass. The wing not shooting the ball rebounds and scores if the shot is missed.

Diagram B: On a make, he quickly steps out of bounds, away from under the backboard, establishes a good angle and throws a deep outlet pass to the middle man who has moved to the sideline in the direction of the shooter. The outlet man catches the pass with his back to the sideline to establish a better view of the entire court when he receives the ball. Players then run outside the lines to the other end as another group of three players runs the drill. Each time, players rotate clockwise to repeat the drill which gives each player a chance to play each of the three positions. We then put the ball in the other wing and repeat the drill. The drill can be run shooting spot-up, backboard or corner jump shots on the break.

Diagram C: We can place a coach or a player pressuring the outlet pass after a score or in the area of 2 to make him move to meet the outlet pass, establish a passing lane and then turn and look up court to the other eight or nine players (offense and defense) once he has received the pass. The drill also can be run with each group doing four to six repetitions.

Diagram D: We run two repetitions full court up and back in the same drill with a slight wrinkle. After crossing the midcourt line with the ball, 2 dribbles across outside the elbow towards the sideline, clearing 3 out and having him screen for 1 who breaks to the corner to receive a pass from 2. Our normal rule is the ball side cutter always sets the screen when wings cross. 3 then can clear out to the opposite or weak side corner, post-up back to the ball after 1's cut or turnout. 3 can set an up block for 2 after he passes to 1 in the corner. The coach should determine which option to run on the return until the players understand all the possible options and then the players are free to run any of the available options.

Diagram E: If 2 dribbles directly to the corner, 1 must cut off 3 either up, out diagonally or curl to the weakside corner.

Diagram F: 2 dribbles the wing out to set up lock-and-lob action.

Fast-Break Organization

Fast-Break Organization

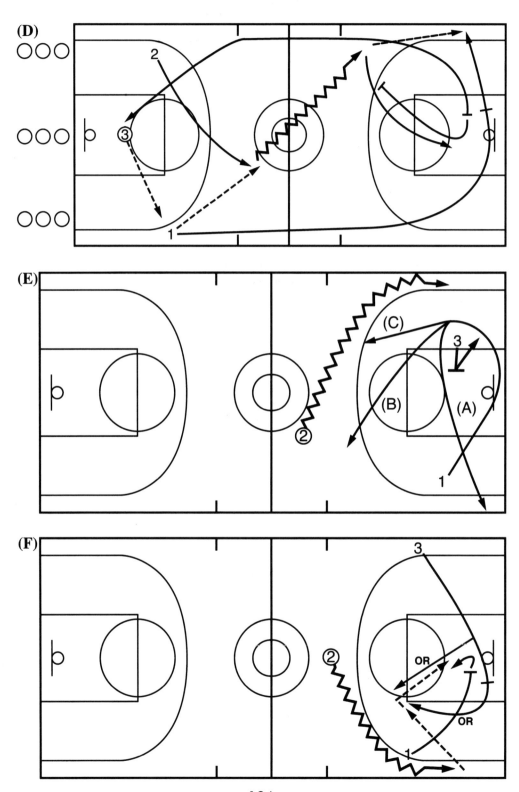

3-Man Fast-Break Organization
(Warm-up drill)

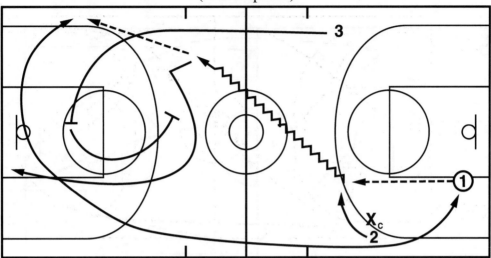

On overplay by the coach, 2 must break to an open area to establish a passing lane for 1.

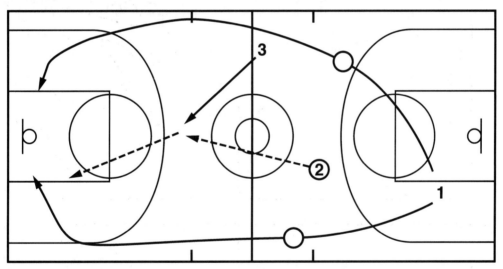

1 has the option of following his pass or going opposite the ball to fill the lane. (We want to read the defense, react and not be predictable.) We also want to push the ball up the court, dribble and/or pass ahead to a free teammate instead of passing the ball behind us. It is also imperative that we run wide to spread the court and the defense.

3-Man Fast-Break Organization
(Warm-up drill)

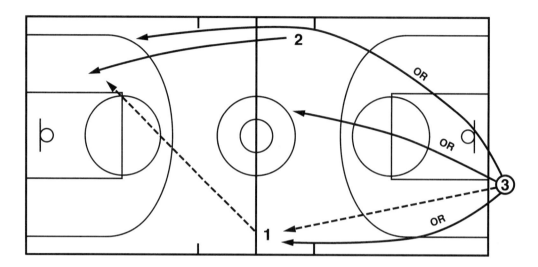

We also practice taking the ball out of bounds quickly after a score and inbounding up the floor on either wing above the free-throw line and along the sideline. The farther the inbounds pass is made the more quickly we begin our fast break or early offense by immediately putting pressure on the defense.

Wings Crossing on the Fast Break
(Diagrams explain the end of the break on the half court)

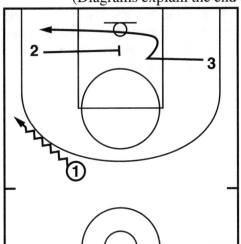

First the wings run for layups. If that isn't possible, we'd prefer the point man declare a side.

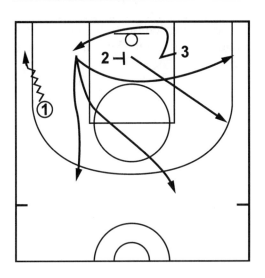

The wing on that side (2) sets a screen for the other wing (3) to avoid confusion. If 1 is below the foul line, 3 curls or circles 2 or makes a vertical or diagonal cut up the lane. On the latter two cuts he can screen (back pick) and step up for the next trailing offensive player 2 must empty out after screening and establish a passing lane.

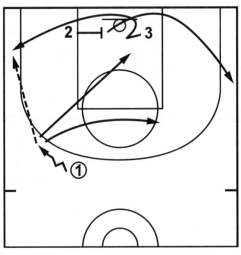

Since 3 gets to the corner before 1, we can pass to him and cut or post 2 who may come back to the ball after screening 3. 2 can also clear out to the weak side of the court or he can set a vertical or diagonal back pick above either elbow.

Wings Crossing on the Fast Break

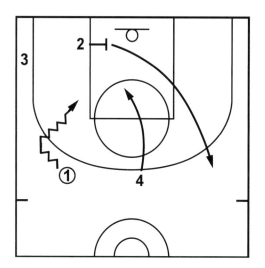

If both 2 and 3 cross, 4 may dive to the goal or we can run the next man down to either block or have the point man drive the ball to the goal.

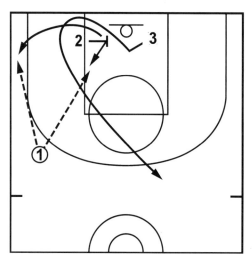

This diagram demonstrates 2 screening 3 and 3 turning out. We can post 2 or 2 can step out for an isolation play and/or open the block for the next player down the court.

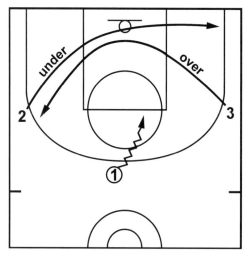

If the point has the ball in the middle of the court, we always designate one wing (left) to cut under 5 (right) over (avoids collisions).

■ Unless you encourage your wings to cross on the break, it is pretty difficult to ask them to run for layups. Crossing on the baseline moves the defense, forcing them to make decisions.

Fast-Break Organization Drill
(Three-man weave, full court)

The coach determines whether we make three, four or five passes with two hands. Begin off a rebound, follow the pass. The wings must first fake away and the wing on the ball side comes back. You can go up and back one, two, three or four times. Have players repeat the drill if they commit errors or miss layups. This drill develops passing skills and helps conditioning. You can also put up two or three minutes on the clock and have your players make 20 or 30 layups without errors in the allotted time.

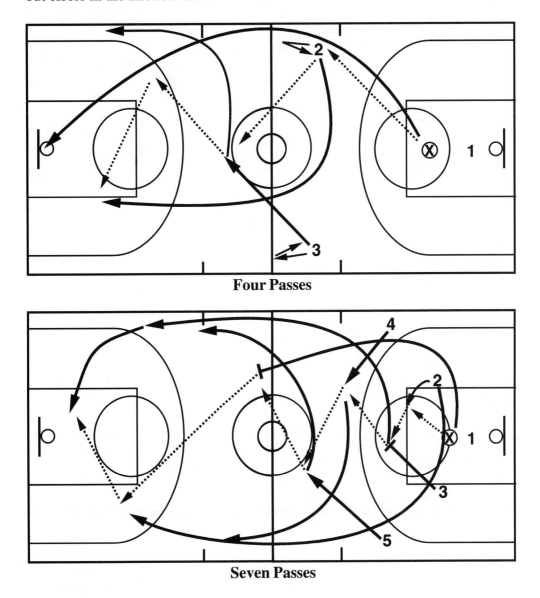

Four Passes

Seven Passes

Makes the drill more interesting and makes the players concentrate more. Errors cause them to repeat the drill.

Fast-Break Organization
(Inside-out drill)

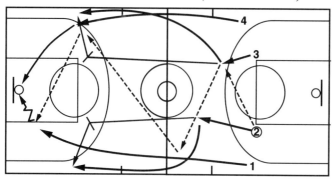

Four lanes, inside out to spread the court. Full court, up and back twice or more times with no misses or errors. Players play both inside and outside positions alternating each time they run full-court. We advance the ball without dribbles and don't permit the ball to hit the floor unless dribbling to cover distance for a layup.

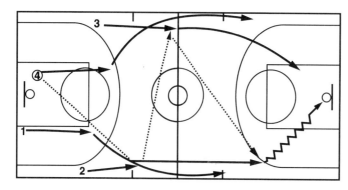

Inside players become outside players and outside players become inside players. Long pass for a layup as well as an outlet. We try to eliminate our dribbles and require the players to run full out on the break. 1 shoots, 4 rebounds and outlets to 2. 2 passes to 3 for a layup and rebounds and outlets. Inside men become outside men after they shoot and outside men become inside men. We run for layups, cover distance on the pass and don't permit the ball to hit the floor. If there are any errors, we repeat the drill. We go up and back 2, 4, 6 or 8 times.

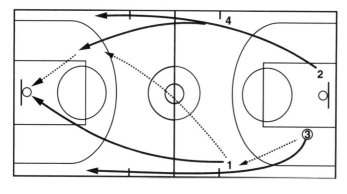

Fast-Break Organization
(Two lines, two balls, two groups)

The rebounder and outlet man run different two-man game options. Pass and cut. Fake, dribble, drive. Screen-and-roll. Dribble handoff, post up. (Any two-man option the coach desires.) We rebound, pass and follow our outlet pass. The outlet man dribbles the length of the court and passes to a wing to set up a two-man game option. At the other end of the court the players switch positions.

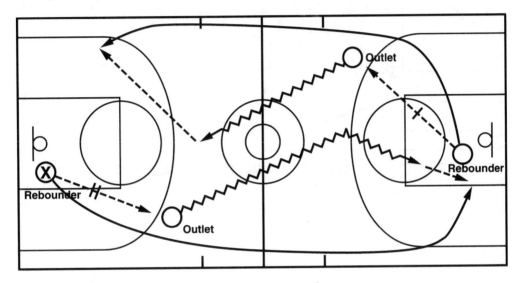

Fast-Break Drill
(Three-lane jump-shooting drill and conditioner)

Each group must make three or four jump shots before the next group replaces them. We mix players (big and small). The coach determines if the shots are banked or not banked and are shot off one dribble or no dribbles (players must sprint to the spot and get there before the ball). This is very good for teaching the quick transition from defense to offense, as well as conditioning and shooting under pressure. You can also shoot three-point shots as a group if the coach so determines. Each player shoots during the drill. The player throwing the last pass before the shot rebounds the ball and the shooter becomes the outlet man and rebounder fills the lane opposite the shooter since he becomes the next shooter. Shots must be taken in an area outside and approximately above or parallel to the elbow area.

R-Rebounder: Passes to the outlet and follows his pass.

O-Outlet: Passes to the shooter, rebounds the shot and passes to the outlet, follows his pass and becomes the next shooter.

S-Shooter: Shoots and becomes the next outlet man and rebounder.

This drill can be run for five to 10 minutes.

Fast-Break Drill
(Three-lane jump-shooting drill and conditioner)

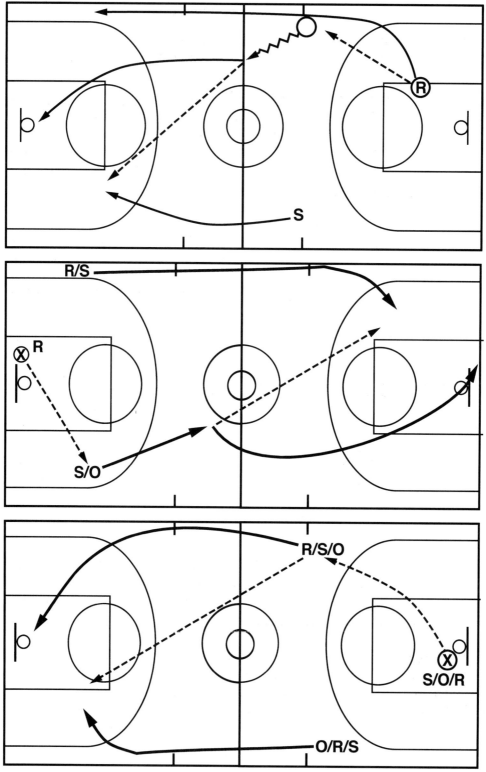

Teaching Offensive Execution and Defending 2 against 1 on the Half Court

(Two offensive vs. one defensive player)

Offensive players' goal is to score a layup or easy opportunity basket by splitting the defender (17-20 feet apart) and keeping the ball off the floor.

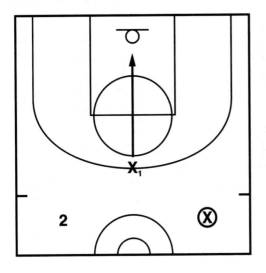

The defender should not turn his back on the ball and should retreat and contain the offense until defensive help arrives. He should fake at them, keep his position in a "V" between both players and not allow a layup or three-point play. (V in front of and below both offensive players.) Fake and retreat moving backward. He cannot permit an offensive player to get behind him and he should try to force them to make an extra pass and pass back, rather than forward, as he contains them and waits for help.

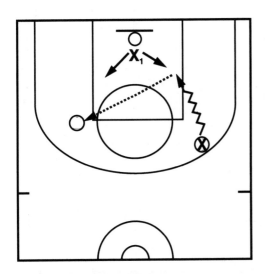

Here, the lone defender buys time until defensive help arrives, move his hands and becomes taller and wider the closer he gets to the basket in an attempt to cut down the passing lanes. He should contest any shot at the goal, look for the offensive foul, and make sure if he fouls, he doesn't give his opponents a three-point play. He also should not go for the steal and give up an easy basket. The shooter becomes the next defender and we have two more offensive players begin passing at midcourt.

Point of emphasis: Force the offense to throw the pass back away from the goal and retreat to the goal by back pedaling, never losing sight of the ball and the two offensive players. Pivot and retreat with your hands up. Don't turn your back and keep yourself at the point of the "V" between the two attacking offensive players.

Teaching Tandem Defense
(To defend the 3-on-2 fast break)

It is a good idea to first set up, explain and demonstrate defensive slides and responsibilities on the half court. We do not want to permit an uncontested layup or a three-point play. The defense's primary responsibility is to stop and contain the ball until help arrives. Ideally, we want to force the offense to pick up their dribble or make extra passes.

The first two defenders back must set up one in front of the other in a tandem defense, not side by side. We prefer the smaller player on top, nearest the ball and the taller player back and closer to the goal.

The role of the top defender is to stop and/or contain the ball out on the floor by faking at the dribbler and slowing him down. Our aim is to have the dribbler pick-up his dribble.

The back defender is responsible for picking up and stopping the player receiving the first wing pass over midcourt. He also tries to force the wing toward his help (the top man) by not getting beat sideline or baseline and by stopping penetration for an easy layup. He does not want to go out and commit too high on the wing, however. He must be under control to force the player with the ball to shoot a jump shot, pick up his dribble or make an extra pass. We want to force the man with the ball to dribble toward our retreating top defender who has released back to deny the crosscourt or penetrating pass and to box out for the weakside rebound. If the ball is passed back out to the middle man, both players immediately return to their original tandem defensive positions.

Point of Emphasis: Each time they drop back, the defenders must pivot, open up and retreat to the goal. They should never turn their backs on the ball. They must see the ball and have their arms spread as they try to clog the passing lane and deflect passes. They take away the baseline and force the offensive player with the ball to his help.

Teaching Tandem Defense
(To defend the 3-on-2 fast break)

(A) (B) (C) (D) (E) (F)

■ These diagrams depict the defense in relation to the ball.

Full-Court Tandem Defense
(3-on-2 and 2-on-1)

(A)

You can set up a drill beginning with 3-on-2 and then coming back 2-on-1 or you can begin 2-on-1 and come back 3-on-2, whichever you prefer. We begin by dividing the squad into three groups, one group of wings on each sideline, even with the free throw circle and the third group of rebounders under the basket (Diagram A, above). We place two defenders in the midcourt area to begin the drill. A coach shoots the ball and the rebounder retrieves it and throws an outlet pass to either wing and then follows his pass. The wing dribbles to the middle and attacks the defense. If you prefer the sideline break, you might want the wing to pass ahead to the wing on the opposite sideline. The tandem defense is established and both defenders retreat as in our half court exercise. Once a shot is taken, made or the defensive team recovers the ball, the two defensive players become offensive players and the shooter, the man at the foul line or the passer, turns and becomes the one retreating defender in the 2-on-1 situation. (Diagrams B and C, next page) Once a shot is made and/or the defense recovers the ball, we have one of the other three players on the court grab the ball, outlet to one of the wings and follow his pass. The drill then is continuous, never stopping and the two players not involved go to the end of the lines. Two new defensive players then step in.

If we go 2-on-1 and then 3-on-2, the player of the first group, if it is the defender stealing a pass, capturing a rebound or if recovering the ball following a score, whichever of these three grabs the ball, he then outlets to either wing, follows his pass and they attack the two defenders waiting at midcourt, who are setting up in a tandem defense, and then retreating. If they stop the three man break or if the offense scores, the tandem defenders retrieve the ball and attack the farthest offensive player in a 2-on-1 situation and now the drill is again continuous.

Full-Court Tandem Defense
(3-on-2 and 2-on-1)

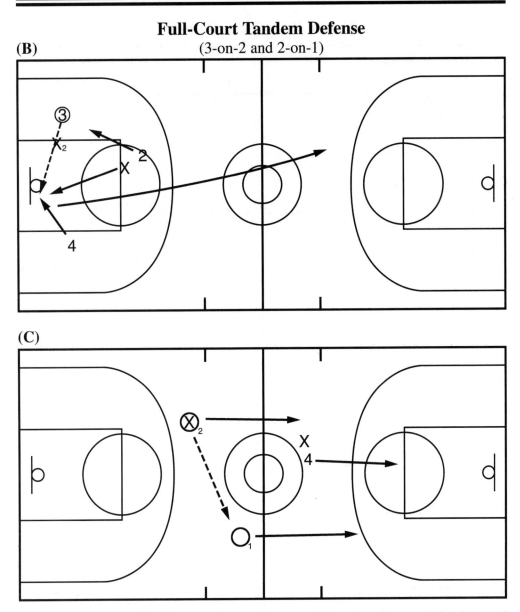

(B)

(C)

We then expand this to 3-on-2 versus 3-on-3 by having the two defenders and anyone of the three offensive players who either grabbed the rebound or got the ball after a score making the transition and attacking two waiting tandem defenders. However, once the ball crosses midcourt, a third trailing defender comes in from behind them at midcourt, picks up a free offensive player in transition and we have a 3-on-3 break. The drill then also becomes continuous as the three defenders then attack two of the three offensive players they just tried to stop and they change from defense to offense and offense to defense. Once over midcourt a third defender steps in and chases. We can then expand the drill and go 4-on-3 with a fourth trailing defender. A hustling player can continually play in the drill if he continues to rebound the ball. All of our fast-break defensive and offensive transition rules are in effect.

2-on-1, 3-on-2 Fast Break

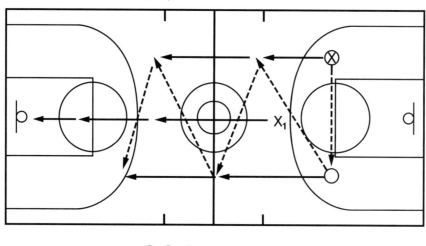

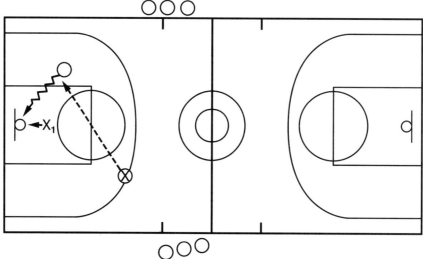

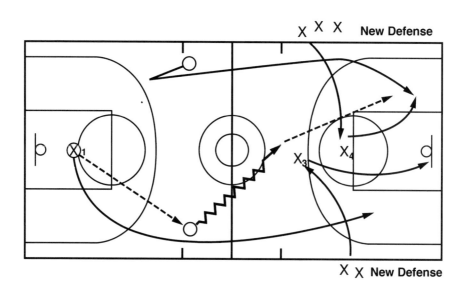

Continuous 11-Man Fast-Break Drill

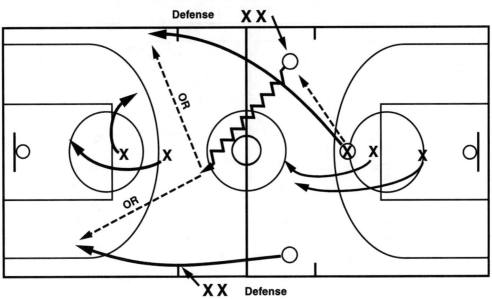

3-on-2 until the ball crosses midcourt when it becomes 3-on-3 as a trailing defender steps in to help. Once the shot is taken, the three defensive men break the other way against two waiting defenders in the offensive end and a trailing defender out of bounds at midcourt again steps in once the ball crosses the 10-second line. Two of the original offensive players become the tandem defenders and the third player goes to one of the mid-court lines. We continue this drill without stopping for five to 10 minutes.

Basketball is a game of mistakes, and the above drill enables the players to make, correct and learn from their mistakes.

We expand our 3-on-2 and 2-on-1 drills to 4-on-3, 3-on-1 and then 5-on-4 and 4-on-2 to help us simulate all types of offensive and defensive fast-break situations. Each drill definitely improves the skills and abilities of our players.

Fast-Break Organization
(4-out and 5-out)

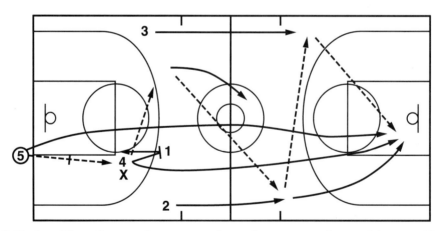

4-Out — Four Lanes with a Trailer. The big man outlets or rebounds each time and passes to the point guard above and outside the free throw circle. The point passes ahead to the wing and the third pass can be returned to the point or ahead to the 3, sprinting for the goal if he is ahead of the field. 5 trails for and must receive the rebound and 2 and 3 cross underneath the goal. On the return, 5 passes to 1 and we run the same break coming back. We go up and back twice or even three or four times with the 5 rebounding each time. On the last basket he shoots the ball as he fills the middle lane as the trailer as the point man opens up a lane for him.

5-Out — Five players, the same as 4-out, but now we have a big man (4 or 5) inbound to the other big man who has screened the point man and stepped back to the ball as a pressure release. Our wings sprint out wide and we try to push the ball ahead for a fast break layup. The wings cross and/or the big men rebound and we go back the other way. If a big man can get out and into the break, we encourage it. He should beat his man down the court. We again go up and back at least twice and the final time the last big man is again the trailer. At times as a conditioner, the same unit goes up and back three or four times in a row without committing an error.

Transition Principles

Develop and then explain your philosophy to your team

When the offensive team has a man advantage (2-on-1, 3-on-2, 3-on-1), that constitutes a fast break. If both teams have equal numbers, the time it takes from getting out of your defensive set, grabbing the rebound (or inbounding the ball after a made shot) and getting into your set offense is the transition game where you might run your early offense or secondary break. It also is the time it takes to go from your defensive set to your offensive set.

Some coaches like to hurry the ball down the court 94 feet on every missed shot. Others prefer to hurry after every made basket. Some will hurry on any opportunity. Again, this is an individual coach's choice and may depend on his personnel. When fast breaking we want to force the break, but not the bad shot.

How fast you get into your offense after pushing the ball or how quickly you pick up defensively if the other team is pushing the ball is a decision you as a coach must make. How do you match up and cover? How do you space your offense so you'll always have defensive balance and men back to cover the other team's fast break opportunities? Every offensive play you design should include good defensive balance principles, as well as good rebounding opportunities. You need to talk, help each other pick up free men, level back to the ball and stop the ball quickly when changing from offense to defense. This emphasis should go on every day in practice so that you leave no stone unturned in your quest to develop a winning program.

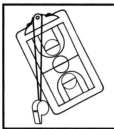

In transition, the first big man back should run straight to the goal, the shortest distance between two points. He should do this on both offense and defense.

Teaching transition basketball

You can devise several drills similar to fast-break drills to teach transition. You can go 3-on-2, and then add a third defender when the ball reaches midcourt. You might go 4-on-3, then add the fourth defender when the ball again reaches midcourt. To be effective in the transition game, you first must beat the opposition down the floor. Set up various offensive and defensive situations. Here you again can practice working both sides of the ball at once. You might want to vary your drills to give different looks. The defense must learn how to stop the break and when and where to pick up offensive players on the floor and the offense must push the ball 94 feet, looking to go inside first and then if nothing is there, going outside and over to change sides with the ball to move the defense.

Offensive and defensive transition

There are several ways to take advantage of offensive transition. You learn to rapidly go from being a defender to an offensive player after getting a steal or forcing a turnover. You can run off a rebound or jump ball and also run off a made free throw or made field goal.

Your players have to work at covering and making the defensive transition in these same situations. You have to talk, hustle and above all expend effort and convert a high percentage of these fast-break opportunities if you are to be a successful and championship caliber team.

Points to emphasize in defensive transition

1. The first man back on defense must cover the goal, talk and contain the offense. He should see the ball and force the opposition to make an extra pass until help arrives. He shouldn't look for the steal at midcourt and permit a layup in transition.

2. The first big man back should pick up the first big man and talk to let his team's other big man know he has to pick up his teammate's man.

3. If someone has picked up your man, get his or another free man in scoring position or in the direction of the help. Don't chase your man and leave another man free.

4. Lock into shooters on transition.

5. Stop the ball. Make the dribbler pick up the ball. Fake at him, but make him pick up the ball. Do whatever you can to stop penetration.

6. Watch out for a defensive man leaking out. Maintain good defensive balance.

7. The first two men back on a break should set up in tandem defense. Practice executing this correctly.

8. In a two-on-one situation, or any situation in which you are outnumbered, force the opposition to make an extra pass. Retreat and cover the goal. Look for a charge.

9. Decide how you want to defend if they spot up in the corners.

10. Decide how you want to defend if they cross on the break. Do you want to switch or stay with your man?

11. Don't run even with your man when the ball is passed ahead. Release and run ahead and get level with the ball providing an opportunity to have a man advantage defensively.

12. Stay level with the ball when playing weakside defense.

13. Retreating big men must help and see the ball. Help stop the dribbler from penetrating and pushing the ball in transition, especially if your opponent trails. Spread yourself wide. Fake at the ball and recover and retreat to the goal.

14. Be aware of opponents running out on our shooters. You need defensive balance.

15. Watch the opposition's big men running the middle of the floor, basket to basket, to post up in an early offense.

16. The first man back in transition can't let them post him. Take away the position your opponent wants. Drive the man off the block or out of the lane. Contain and wait until help arrives.

17. The first man back shouldn't let any offensive player get behind him.

18. When rotating, pick up the free man in the direction of the help.

19. The closer you get to the basket, the bigger you should become to help clog the passing lanes.

20. Bump the big men off the block. Meet them high as long as you are the first man back and no one is behind you.

21. If you are next to the rebounder, you can choke the outlet, play the passing lane to the outlet and pressure the rebounder's pass to delay or stop the fast break, especially if he is your man.

22. Keep the ball in front of you in the full-court defensive transition.

23. Make sure you match up correctly when your team is shooting a free throw. Know who you must guard.

24. The first big man back must hustle to cover the goal so the other big man can trap at midcourt with the point man in transition.

25. Don't run out on transition before you have the rebound.

26. Trailing defenders must look to pick up shooters in transition.

27. Try to eliminate or deter ball reversal.

Points to remember in transition offense

1. The fifth man in a break must stay back to defend.

2. Force the break, not the bad shot.

3. Keep the dribble in front of you so they can't steal the ball from behind.

4. Always pass the ball ahead to the free man.

5. Don't pass the ball back on the break unless no other option exists. Keep pressure on the defense.

6. Look for the step-up blind pick-and-roll if the dribbler is being pressured and you have a good angle on the ball.

7. Make your outlet pass long, above the free-throw line and preferably toward the sideline.

8. Go 94 feet. In, out and over, and reverse the ball. Change sides with the ball when establishing your early offense.

9. Watch opponent's big men overplaying outlet passes after a basket or rebound by faking up court and spinning in a surprise move to intercept. Receivers must establish passing lanes.

10. Teach your 3, 4 and/or 5 men to run the middle of the floor to the goal in transition. Teach them to post up, get behind the defense and get easy baskets in the lane. The first man to get there controls and has a right to the area.

11. The point guard should pass and cut and you should try to reverse the ball to him if the fast break isn't available.

■ Remember: The team making the best transitions from offense to defense and from defense to offense usually emerges victorious.

 Use the dribble to advance the ball, penetrate, cover distance and get out of trouble. Run with your dribble and penetrate when practicing how to beat your opponent one-on-one.

Transition Drill
(Up and back, 3-on-3, 4-on-4 or 5-on-5)
Objective: Making the transition from offense to defense.

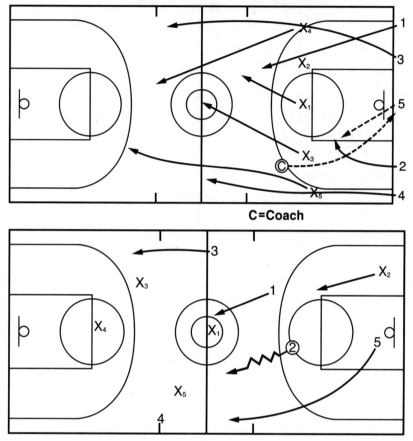

C=Coach

The coach throws the ball to one of the offensive players on the baseline and at the same time calls the name of one of the defensive players. The defensive player he calls must run and touch the near baseline while the offense begins to fast break and the defense retreats to cover the basket, pick up their men (or the player closest to the basket) and try to slow up, contain or stop the ball, buying time until the player whose name was called can recover and get back on defense to pick up his own or a teammate's free man. We want our defensive players to level back even with the ball to pick up the ball and the free men closest to the basket. It is important that the player whose name was called not go back to his man if he is covered, thus leaving another man free. Players must talk and call out the players they pick up in transition to eliminate confusion.

We then expect the offensive team to look for the fast break and if not there, move the ball, call a play and execute. The defense must reform, organize and stop them. If the offensive team scores, we switch places and run the same drill from that basket or we have previously instructed both teams to fast break the opposite way off a rebound or steal or to take the ball out quickly after a score and run our offensive transition the opposite way. We want to prevent easy baskets when outnumbered in defensive transition.

157

Press Offense and Defense

(3 out or 4 out)

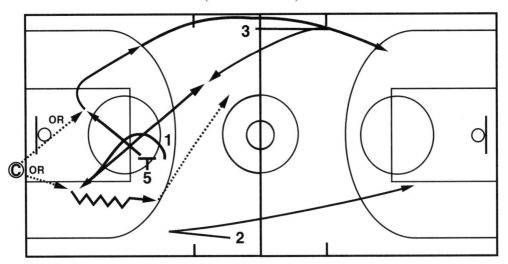

Begin 3-on-3 and build to 4-on-4.

Coach inbounds. The point runs off a pick by the post man and tries to get free. If the point is doubled, the big man comes to the ball as an outlet. If not, once the ball is inbounded the coach determines if the big man trails, goes wide or runs the middle of the floor. The wings begin at midcourt and fake to the ball and go long or fake long and come to the ball to break the pressure by posting from the weak side to the middle. We then run full-court transition, looking for the fast break or our early offense options.

We practice press offense 3-on-3, 4-on-4 and then 5-on-5 as we inbound and run looking to score off our early offense or transition.

Coaches can run their secondary break or press offense without permitting dribbling or by limiting the offense to one dribble, etc., until they cross midcourt. This helps concentration, learning, timing, execution and conditioning.

It is also a good idea to practice your press offense against six or seven defenders to help build your players' confidence when attacking pressure defenses.

Offensive

Drills

Each of these drills should be tailored to the coach's offensive philosophy and schemes. Build your offense step by step. Do what works best for you.

2-on-0

Create your drills utilizing different options: pass-and-cut (inside or away), pass-and-bury (inside or away), pass-and-screen, pass-and-replace, pass-and-get ball back, dribble/hand off, dribble man out, dribble to post.

3-on-0

Expand the drills to include pass-and-cut, pass-and-bury, pass-and-screen away, pass-and-wait for backpick, UCLA downscreen and upblock, diagonal weakside cut to the ball, 3-man weave, pass-and-screen ball, blind step up pick-and-roll, dribble out and screen across lane, curl, fade, flare or counter with weakside movement, dribble handoff, and pick-and-roll options.

4-on-0

You have to integrate your timing and emphasize the importance of proper spacing and have each player understand why he is important in having your offense work smoothly and with maximum efficiency.

Offensive Cuts
(4-on-4)

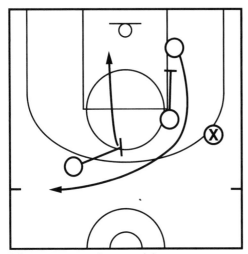

Zipper screendown with counter.

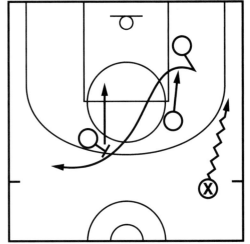

Option zipper screendown with counter.

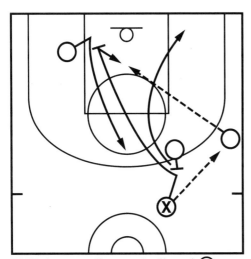

UCLA post diagonal. Guard ⊗ cuts vertically. 5 cuts diagonally after picking for ⊗.

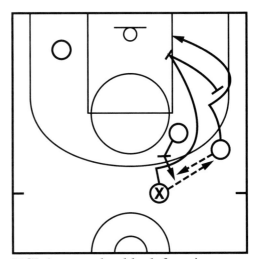

UCLA cut and upblock for wing.

Offensive Cuts
(4-on-4)

Guard-to-guard weakside cut and post-up after the guard comes off of the stack.

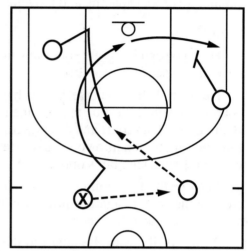

Guard-to-guard, blind pig — second guard around.

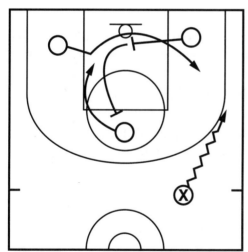

Triangle, pick-the-picker.

High pick-and-roll, step back — diagonal weakside cut to the post.

Set up drills...same as 3-on-0, and pass-and-screen the wing, pass-and-screen the opposite post or corner, have big men screen across, screen stack (double after pass), hit post and spot or cross, create a buddy system (G to G, G to F), emphasize proper spacing and movement.

5-on-0

Here you can integrate your transition offense and player movement to create outstanding scoring opportunities.

Develop drills to run set plays, having five men play with balance and rebounding position alerting the fifth man to his responsibility to defensive balance. Begin on the half court and after a score, quickly inbound the ball and run your full-court transition into your early offense. You can go up and back two or three times and run each play's options.

Each of the following situations and drills should be practiced in different areas of the court to again simulate realistic game situations. You can divide into stations and teach these concepts.

2-on-2 drills from the guard to the wing, guard to the post, across the top from guard to guard and utilizing the pick-and-roll.

When we add a defense, we can begin to have our players actually visualize their responsibilities in helping free one another to create advantageous scoring opportunities. Emphasize your fundamentals, timing and eye communication.

3-on-3

Utilize triangles in your offensive teaching to develop cutting and screening tactics which cause the defense to constantly react to you and causes them to make split-second decisions.

Work on drills in different areas of the full and half court to practice these moves.

Send a cutter to the corner and run splitting the post off the flash post or set up a fake split and go backdoor on an overplay or switch.

4-on-4

Here we can set up shell options offensively.

5-on-5 drills utilizing your full offense

Incorporate and practice options you don't use in your normal offense to help your defensive preparation. By doing this you may find some of these may be effective counters for you to incorporate into your offensive plans. Many times your better offensive players have a knack for knowing how to most effectively maximize an offensive set and they'll teach you something you may have overlooked or neglected to mention.

5-on-5 Half-Court Drill
(Coach is 6th man on offense)

The offensive players move to get free and the coach makes a pass to a player. That player can shoot if he has a good shot or he must pass the ball back to the coach and move by cutting or screening to help a teammate get free. Each team has five opportunities to score. They may rebound their missed shots. The team with more baskets wins. Next you can permit the player receiving the pass from the coach to make a scoring pass to a player who has worked to free himself.

Example of coach passing and offensive players moving without the ball.

Football Game Practice Drill

Competitive five-on-five, half-court or full-court drill. The first team to score 30 points wins the game.

a. Teams huddle up to call plays on offense and defense on each possession.

b. Teams alternate possessions after each stop.

c. Each team has four offensive opportunities to score.

d. Each basket scored is valued at six points.

e. After each score, the player scoring then has the opportunity to shoot a free throw worth one point or he can elect to go one on one versus his defender for two points.

f. This drill teaches initiative and decision making and promotes execution and intensity on offense and defense.

Screening
and Cutting

It may seem basic, but there is a lot to learn about screening and cutting and it should be reviewed. We tell players using a screen that it's better to be late, rather than early if someone is screening for them. If you're late, you can make sure your man is being screened, giving yourself the option of going over or under the screen and to change your speed and direction. Movement off or away from the ball provides the player with the ball the option to penetrate and beat his defender. You want to teach your players how to run the pick-and-roll effectively by sometimes beginning to set the pick, but then slipping it before the defense can react or by slipping it if the defender is on the outside shoulder of the player setting the screen. Dribblers must wait until the pick is set before putting the ball on the floor to effectively take advantage of the defense and eliminate possible offensive fouls. You may want to teach your players how to step back after the player has come off him on the screen and also how to loop in front of the dribbler without setting a screen, thus opening the floor and providing another passing or penetrating option for the man with the ball.

You can also teach your players how to bend their knees, turn and take the brunt of the blow on the pick-and-roll by pivoting, and having the player setting the screen seal the defender with his back, thus creating an easy passing lane and scoring opportunity. Teach your post players to screen across the lane and explain if the defender goes high, the cutter should go low, and if his defender goes low, he should cut high to an open area. If the defenders try to switch, you might teach your players to screen their own defenders or the switcher or to step up,

Screening

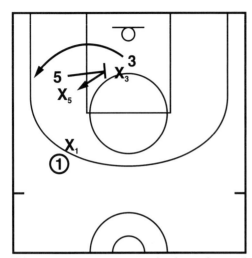 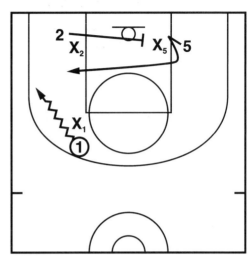

Big man set your screen in the paint and then post back to the ball closer to the basket once your screen has been used.	Wait for the screen deep in the paint on a pindown screen. Set up your man. Run him into the screen. Be late rather than early.

split or slide to the goal. Teach screening from both the weak side and the strong side. Incorporate this with your three-on-three and four-on-four man drills before adding the post player. This develops better timing and spacing and keeps the middle open. Emphasize how good spacing enhances the big man's ability to operate. Work at teaching your players how to recognize and read the defense. When you work a high-low screen, you want to teach them how to screen and come back for the ball. Emphasize this by drilling on the half court and the full court. Demonstrate and set up all your offenses and all of your sets. Work on picking the picker, the lock-and-lob, and the reverse pivot move to the basket when the big man is being overplayed. Continually emphasize that the easiest way to get a shot is to set a screen for someone else! Don't neglect setting multiple screens as well.

Set up schemes and drills with the cutter going to either corner to demonstrate how you can open up the inside by taking away some weakside defensive help.

Have your players read and recognize how they are being played when they are cutting to the ball or using screens. Most defenders are taught to come over the top or slide through from the weak side. By cutting behind the screen to the ball, you may find yourself completely free. Players must always see the ball when cutting to the goal or screening after passing, because they are still a scoring option.

- Backpick option: If a man is closely guarded, set a backpick for him.
- Downscreen option: If the defensive player is sagging off of you, set a downscreen to free your teammate.

Utilize the pick-the-picker option:

1. To screen to get free the simplest and easiest way.

2. To screen your own defender, to eliminate or combat switches and to post and seal your defender.

Combat switching by:

1. Using a brush block to cut early and surprise the defense.

2. Freezing your defender and then cutting.

3. Splitting the defense.

4. Looping to open up the court for the dribbler.

5. Stepping up into the paint toward the ball.

Again, to reiterate:

- In the two-man game, when picking, we backscreen if the man is being closely guarded, or downscreen if he is loosely guarded or playing back.

- We teach: Screen your buddy on the weak side and screen the ball on the strong side of the floor. You can also fake the screen and cut to the goal.

- When you dive to the goal, cut behind the defender if he shows you his back and keep coming to establish a passing lane for a trapped player.

- With the ball on the low post, cut inside the high defender to create a lane enabling you to receive a return scoring opportunity pass or to screen a man coming to double.

- Sometimes a brush block timed correctly is better than an actual physical screen because it catches the defense by surprise.

- Set your screen on the defender's numbers (head hunt).

Rules for the Pick-and-Roll Offense

1. When running the pick-and-roll with the dribble not yet used, the man with the ball can hold it over his head with two hands as a signal for a post man to come and screen the ball.

2. You should not dribble until the screen is set to avoid offensive fouls being called.

3. If they force the pick-and-roll sideline, dive your top man to the goal if his man looks to steal or play the passing lane. If they play the screener tight, you may be able to drive baseline unmolested.

4. If the opponents squeeze and go under the pick-and-roll, we can and should change direction with the dribble and repick.

5. When screening, if the defender is on your outside shoulder, split or slip the pick. Go to the goal.

6. Step up from the low post to screen the wing on the pick-and-roll if the ball handler is being closely guarded.

7. Practice and teach dribblers to stretch or string out the trap or how to split the trap with the dribble.

8. The screener must decide whether to dive to the goal or step back or to the sideline versus a hard show by the defender playing him.

9. Always set a screen by bending your knees and pivoting with the force of the blow when the defender makes contact.

10. If you sense your defender going to trap early, you can create a scoring opportunity by immediately diving to the goal before the double team can take place.

 Leave your feet with the ball thinking shot. Don't leave your feet thinking pass.

Individual

Offense

Good coaches try to utilize each of their players' individual skills and try to keep their drills varied and competitive. We use a lot of shooting drills from a lot of different locations on the floor. Instruct the players what you want them to do.

Meet the pass and:

1. Shoot without the dribble.

2. Fake and shoot.

3. Use one dribble and shoot a jump shot.

4. Fake, use two dribbles and shoot a jump shot.

5. Fake and drive to the basket with one dribble.

6. Fake and drive to the basket with two dribbles.

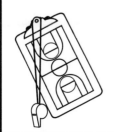

The last dribble before a shot should be a high, hard or quick explosive dribble to help you quickly get into your shot.

169

Do each exercise for a couple of minutes so each player works on each offensive skill. You should also do some full-court individual drills, including dribbling the ball up the floor, changing direction, crossing over, etc. This is important for every player, regardless of size or position. Every player should have time to work on his ballhandling every day and it is the coach's duty to provide and devote practice time to honing these skills and building confidence. Two minutes of dribbling will benefit all of your players in this manner.

Teach players that when they penetrate and leave their feet, they should always think "shoot" before "pass." If they're thinking shot, they can always pass the ball, but if they are thinking pass first, it's very difficult to shoot the basketball effectively and with the proper balance.

Players should be looking for opportunity shots in their rhythm and range with the board covered.

Passing the Basketball

Create drills that make your players aware of the importance of passing effectively to help the offensive player score and also of faking and passing under pressure from a single defender or double team. A good drill to teach passing is "Monkey in the Middle" or two offensive players vs. one defensive player.

An inbounder, before receiving the ball from the referee, should be instructed to step back from the sideline or baseline to create a better passing angle, better vision and relieve pressure.

Make sure you know which player can inbound the ball near the end of a game. You may need another passer if you are being pressured. You never know who will be available at the end of a game because of foul problems or injuries so work with all of your players on inbounding the basketball. Learn which players are most comfortable and have good judgment when inbounding the ball.

Teach your players that they can run the baseline to inbound the ball after a basket when being pressured. The inbounder should count to himself so he is aware of the five-second violation rule when inbounding the ball.

Offensive Shooting Drills
(With two or three basketballs)

We do these drills at both baskets (stations) simultaneously by dividing up the squad and using coaches or other players as passers. We practice taking the shots our offense gets us during a game. Players must follow, rebound and put back misses. You can set up any number of options, either horizontally, vertically or diagonally, as well as up, down or out. We do the same drill for the pick-and-roll. The dribbler has one ball as he comes off the screen and if he shoots, the coach passes to the screener, and if he passes, the coach passes to the passer. Use both sides of the court. We really place a great deal of emphasis on timing and spacing in all of our two ball shooting drills.

Shooting Drills
(2 balls, 3 players)

This probably is one of the very best shooting drills to develop and practice spot shooting, penetrating and shooting off one or two dribbles and catching, faking and shooting; catching, dribbling, faking and shooting and following your shots. We divide the squad into two groups (big men at one basket and small men at the other basket) and each group alternates every two exercises and does the following:

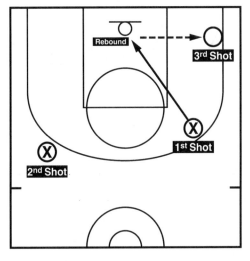

1. Two men alternate shooting and following their shots. Jump shots without the dribble. They rebound their shot and throw it back to the player in their group without a ball.

2. Jump shots with one dribble.

3. Jump shots with two dribbles or a crossover or change of pace and direction dribble.

4. One dribble, stop, ball fake, jump shots.

5. It is important that players take shooting drills seriously and work with game intensity when practicing.

After the first group of three does 1 and 2 above, we bring the second group in to do the same and then the first group does 3 and 4. We use the clock and give each group 1½ minutes for each exercise. We emphasize:

a. Shots from different spots.

b. Running and covering distance with the dribble.

c. The last dribble before a shot being a high, hard, explosive dribble.

This drill can be done every day in practice.

171

Pick-and-Roll Options

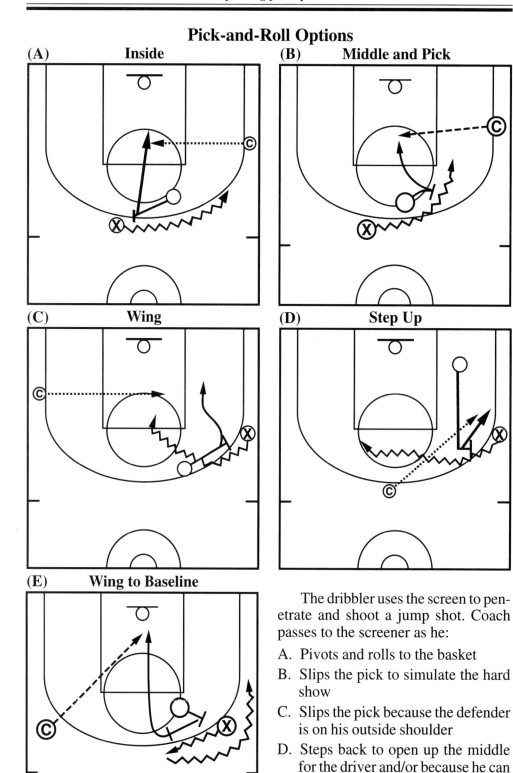

(A) **Inside**

(B) **Middle and Pick**

(C) **Wing**

(D) **Step Up**

(E) **Wing to Baseline**

The dribbler uses the screen to penetrate and shoot a jump shot. Coach passes to the screener as he:

A. Pivots and rolls to the basket

B. Slips the pick to simulate the hard show

C. Slips the pick because the defender is on his outside shoulder

D. Steps back to open up the middle for the driver and/or because he can shoot the ball

E. Repicks if the defense hugs or squeezes and goes under

Offensive Shooting Drills
(With two basketballs)

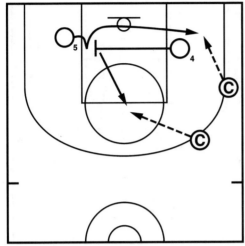

A. Screen across the lane and pivot to the ball. When O5 cuts over the top of the screen by O4, O4 rolls back to the ball on the low side.

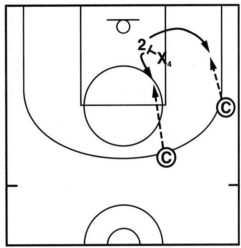

B. Turn out and post to the ball or slip for a lob pass. 2 must read 4's defender as well as his own, because he may decide to cut over the top of 4 in order to free himself for a shot instead of turning out.

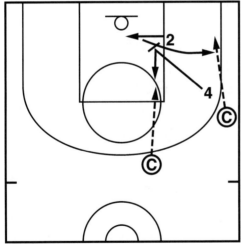

C. Pin down and post up.

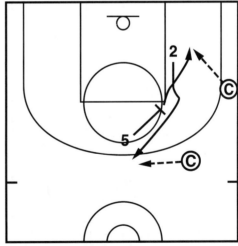

D. Zipper counter and post to the ball. We teach 2 to set up his man. He may go under 5's screen after two or three times or he may fake up, double back and post his man. If 2 posts or goes backdoor, 5 must read and adjust his cut.

Offensive Shooting Drills
(With two basketballs)

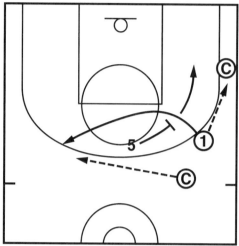

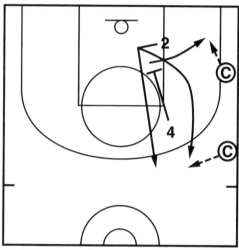

E. Loop and dive to the post. Here, we have 1 pass to the coach and loop under 5 in a pressure release.

F. Zipper and post up. Vertical pin-down 4 on 2. 2 must wait for the screen and cut quickly to the top. We also have 2 backpick 4 in this drill.

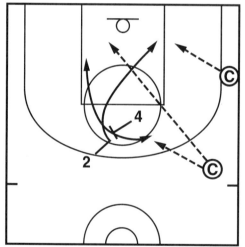

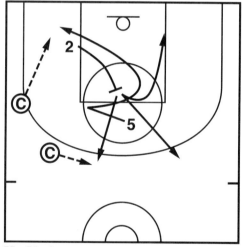

G. Hawk cut and post up. 2 uses a screen by 4 to diagonally cut to the post or corner. 4 steps to the ball or fakes out and goes to the goal for the lob. 2 can also cut and backpick 4.

H. Utah cut and step out. 2 diagonally backpicks 5 who dives to the post as 2 steps to the ball. 2 can fake the backpick and roll for the lob pass.

Many other options are also available and should be tailored to a team's offensive needs and options.

Rebounding

Create a team and individual mentality

The mentality of every player should be to anticipate a miss on every shot both offensively and defensively. Each player should consider himself a rebounder and pursue each rebound on offense and defense. (You may designate one or two players to stay back to defend the transition, and not crash the board, but they still should be responsible for capturing long rebounds, if possible. If an opposing player is assigned to leak out on a jump shot for a possible fast break, the shooter should not go to the defensive board.) Players have to get themselves into a position to capture rebounds. Be aware if it's a hard shot or soft shot. Realize if it's a shot from the corner or straight on. Always follow the flight of the ball while it's in the air. Play the percentages. Know when your teammates are likely to shoot. That might give you a split second advantage over your defender in getting to the board. Work to get into position. You must box out. Make contact, put a body on a man and get between him and the basket, whether you are under the basket or 20 feet out. It's been said that the best rebound is one that hits the floor: That means your team had everyone sealed out. You should also be active even if you can't grab a rebound. Tap it out to a predesignated position so your teammates can capture and control the loose rebound. Remember, often times it is the little things that win basketball games, and you must concentrate on these things.

Teaching rebounding

Set up drills. Work on boxing out. Make it a challenge so that if you get the offensive rebound, you continue to play offense. Make your drills competitive

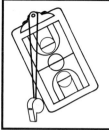

All five players must consider themselves rebounders.

and meaningful. When you are scrimmaging, reward a team if it doesn't allow an offensive rebound for a certain period of time. Remember, the most dangerous offensive rebounder is the player taking the shot and the shooter must be boxed out!

Offensive rebounding

Teach your players to crash the boards. It's tough to box out a player coming hard from the weak side or top of the key directly to the board, especially if he has a running start. If they get boxed out, you have to teach the players how to step back and get around the defender by breaking the contact. Players have to anticipate the miss and the direction of the rebound. They can't just stand there and hope the ball will ricochet into their hands. Keep your eye on the ball. Long shots create long rebounds.

Defensive rebounding

The most important thing to work on is boxing out or at least making contact on every shot. Look to make contact no matter where you are on the court or who you are closest to, you must get yourself between that player and the basket — every time a shot is taken. It takes determination, hustle and strength, but every player must be committed to pursuing and rebounding the basketball.

On foul shots, teach your players that they should box out the other player's legs. Make contact and get a body on them early to keep them from crossing over the lane or ducking behind you on the baseline. And it goes without saying that the defender closest to the foul shooter must step in front of the shooter every time or pinch the rebounder if you give boxing the shooter responsibilities to a player outside the lane.

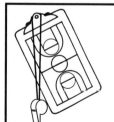

Box and board. Make contact, see the ball and rebound.

Rebounding Rules

1. Don't give second-shot opportunities.

2. Box out and make contact.

Photo©Frank McGrath

Strong Rebound

3. If boxed out, step back, move and break the contact.

4. You can offensive rebound from behind the defender by hiding on the baseline, stepping out of bounds and coming in on the other side to rebound. There is no rule against this if you step inbounds with both feet first before touching the ball. Don't let them put a body on you.

5. Tap out rebounds you can't control or grab to a designated area, perhaps the elbows or the foul line. Alert your players to this possibility so they can capture loose rebounds.

6. Box out on defensive free throws. No second shots.

7. Be aware of weakside rebounders stepping out of bounds and then stepping in from behind to rebound.

8. On free throws, keep your feet together for a larger step. Also stay closer to the man or farther away from the man you are trying to beat so he'll need a longer step to box you out.

9. Fight for position. Don't let them box you out. Move constantly.

10. Rebound effectively and stop your opponents' fast breaks.

11. Box out the shooter. He is the most dangerous offensive rebounder. He knows where the miss will bounce.

12. After switching, concentrate on boxing out and putting bodies on people.

13. Offensive rebounders can cross and screen for each other to cause men boxing out to make decisions and turn their heads.

14. Follow the flight of the ball as it leaves the shooter's hand to determine where it might land.

15. The longer the shot, the longer the rebound.

Tap loose balls, rebounds or deflections to a predesignated area so your teammates can run them down. Don't tap them under your opponent's offensive goal.

Incorporating Post Play

Every offense should include options that take the ball inside to the post. A good way to teach this is by requiring that during practice one out of every three passes made must go inside to the post. It's important to have proper spacing so that it becomes difficult to double-team the post player until he receives the ball. Your ball handlers and other players have to recognize different defenses and must be able to set screens to get the post player open to receive the ball. Work on the lock and lob, the fake screen, stepping into the ball and the high-low or reverse pivot for a dunk if the post is three-quartered and overplayed or if your defender is playing above you. This again requires establishing and emphasizing the importance of eye contact between the players involved in this action.

Set up drills utilizing the single and double post, a high post and a low post, and demonstrate how post men can help create offensive opportunities by moving and screening for each other. Run these drills with defensive as well as offensive players. Get your post players used to learning how to play against individual defenders in order to build their confidence. This will help your players recognize where their defenders are when they play with their backs to the basket. Utiliize any of your players regardless of size if they are adept at the post-up game.

Rules for Teaching Post Offense

1. Many times it is a good idea to hit a man flashing to the low post on the move when he is a step ahead of the defender instead of when he stops and the defender is already playing him.

2. When fronted on the low post, step over the front foot of your defender to seal him and get free.

3. Double low-post offense: a) When the ball is in the hands of the point guard at the top of the circle, the big men on the blocks should duck in; b) when the ball is on the wings, the big man nearest the ball should screen across or step up and out and screen on the ball if he can't get good post-up position.

4. You must practice and teach your post men how to combat traps from different areas of the court.

5. Teach your post men to turn and face and/or make their move before the trap is set.

6. Teach them to pass before the trap can be established and not only once they are pressured.

7. Teach big men to receive in the post, throw back out and again demand the ball as they repost and get better position closer to the goal.

8. Teach them when passing out of a trap, to split the trap after the pass and to chase the ball providing an outlet for the receiver.

9. Work on the lock-and-lob or high-low if the post is fronted or three-quartered too high on the floor.

10. Big men should break the contact and run by or below the defensive post to the baseline when they are met high and challenged or denied position. They can then break back to the ball in good scoring position.

11. Post players can fake a pass and go up and under before the trap is set.

12. Big men must curl to establish passing lanes for each other when one defensive big man helps double the ball or tries to block a shot.

13. The dribbler should dribble below the foul line on the wing to create a passing angle for the player fronted or three-quartered on the high post. This enables the offensive man to seal his defender and reverse for the lob.

14. Teach big men to back the defender down with the dribble when they play behind him.

15. Post players should recognize when the wing is overplayed so they can flash post and create a backdoor opportunity or a pressure release.

16. Designate a big man to inbound the ball after a basket unless a guard or wing has just made a breakaway basket.

17. Hit the post and cut, spot, split, screen away or bury.

18. Protect the ball. Don't bring it down where guards can swipe it.

19. Work on quick ball fakes and getting the defender off his feet to draw fouls and create three-point play scoring opportunities.

20. Present a target to the passer and meet the pass. Establish strong post position.

21. Establish wide, balanced position on the low post.

22. Post and repost to relieve defensive pressure. When reposting, try to position yourself closer to the basket. Fake away and come back.

23. Step up to meet passes, especially when they are playing your outside shoulder. Receive, pivot, turn and face the basket and attack.

24. Weakside post men should step up the lane when we have an offensive post-up mismatch to take away the help or double-team.

25. A low post big man should follow or chase the dribbler along the baseline when we run the middle pick-and-roll to provide room for the screener to roll to the goal.

26. Protect the ball when you bring it up to shoot. Many inside players try to stop or block shots when two hands come to the ball.

27. Loop to help free men driving to the goal.

28. You can run the UCLA options with the post man stepping up and setting the high post screen.

29. Weakside post men must step up when another offensive player drives toward the goal. Establish a passing lane, especially on baseline drives when your defender goes to help or double-team.

 When practicing your shot, sometimes stop and ball fake after you stop your dribble and before you shoot. This fake may lose your defender or make him leave his feet and foul you. You'll also be practicing and simulating game situations.

181

Post Offense

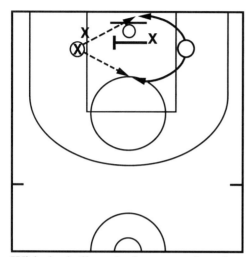

With the ball on the low post, the other post man must step up to provide a passing lane should his defender trap or double the post. This gives him a great lane to crash, rebound or receive a scoring pass. He can curl to an open area in the lane or sneak baseline behind the defense to achieve the same purpose.

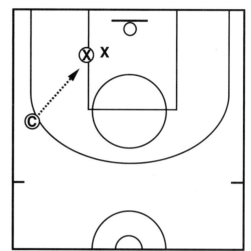

The coach passes to the player in the low post, then the post man plays 1-on-1 with or without a dribble. The post man can work on all types of shots and if not comfortable pass the ball back to the coach and repost to establish better position.

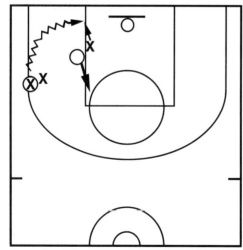

On a baseline drive, the offensive post man must step up the lane to create room and a passing lane for the driver.

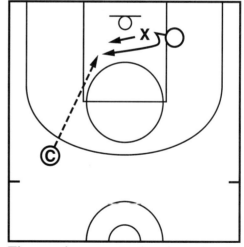

The coach passes to the player breaking to the post. Then he goes 1-on-1 with or without the dribble. We predetermine whether or not we permit the post man to dribble.

Photo©Frank McGrath

Getting position in the post

Half-Court Defensive Post Drill
(5 offensive players vs. 4 defenders — 3 perimeter and 1 post defender)

As each pass around the perimeter is made, the defense pressures the ball and the players off the ball step toward the pass and step back almost level with the ball to help deny passing lanes to the post players. Our normal defensive rules, with the dribble alive, apply. We deny the penetrating pass, in the "ball-you-man" principle. We slough off the ball and to the middle from the weak side and we front the post (Diagram A).

A. Ball at top. We three-quarter or front the post.

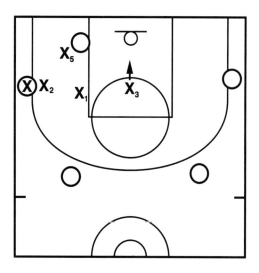

B. Ball below the free-throw line. We front the post, pressure the ball and support down and toward the ball from the top and weak side.

Half-Court Defensive Post Drill
(5 offensive players vs. 4 defenders — 3 perimeter and 1 post defender)

C. Wing baseline drive. We front the post and double the driver with post defender X5. X1 chases dribbler to inside. X2 sinks down and rotates back as X3 helps on the post man. (If X2 gets there first, X3 plays 2, 3 or 4.)

D. Ball on the post. Each perimeter player sloughs back, off their men and tries to dig ball out of the post without fouling.

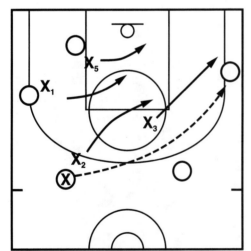

E. On a cross court pass, all defenders move while the ball is in the air, in the direction of the pass as they rotate back to help. The man nearer the ball must run to pressure it, but he must be under control to stop penetration and contest the shot.

F. Movement versus dribble penetration. Players off the ball move down and in the direction of the ball to help rotate and support their teammates.

Photo©Frank McGrath

Defending in the post

Big Man Drill

(6-4-2)

Semicircle of three passers with a big man on offense with his back to the basket. He meets the pass, turns and faces, and makes a strong move to the basket, using only one or two dribbles (as determined by the coach). If he makes the shot, it counts as one basket. If he misses and grabs the rebound before it hits the floor and puts it back in, it is also a point. The last one or two shots in each group must be dunked. Each player makes six and then another player replaces him. The next player makes four and so on.

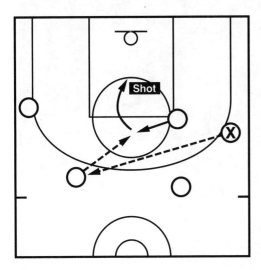

Players as passers rotate and become shooters until each player has completed 6-4-2. You can, of course, increase the repetitions, i.e., 8-6-2 or 10-8-4. This a great drill for teaching and practicing offensive moves, rebounding your own missed shots and building strength and stamina.

Photo©Frank McGrath

Double-Teaming

Combating Special Defensive Techniques

You should have your team prepared for any occurrence. If the defense tries to double-team from the front, explain how you want to break that defense. If they are set to trap from in front or from behind, explain how you want to utilize and position your players to combat this tactic.

How do you combat them fronting the post? What do you do if they force the ball to the middle or to the sideline? How do you combat doubling the dribbler from behind? Your players must know what to do if they jump switch on screens or use other surprise or unorthodox tactics.

Anticipate facing each of these situations and work against them in practice. Think about and practice against how you'll handle an opponent double-teaming your best shooter in critical situations, what you'll do to free him and what other options you'll have available to you. Create your own drills to help your players respond to difficult or different defensive situations.

Combating, Attacking and Breaking the Trap

Set up game situations in practice. Set up the different traps that might be used. Teach the players off the ball what their responsibilities are. Explain how it is their job to create open passing lanes to the ball and which players you want to dive to the goal. The trapped players must know when to get rid of the ball and what tactics they can use to take advantage of the double-team. Show them where to look for their outlets and how to pivot and pass when they are trapped. Practice this without the actual trap, as well as against trapping defenders. You can use six defenders instead of five when you want to teach your players how to handle pressure.

You must teach the trapped player what to do when he passes the ball out of a trap. A lot of players will throw a pass, relax and figure that their job is done instead of reacting properly to free themselves. Teach your players without the ball how they must create passing lanes and how the trapped player can recognize those lanes. Teach them how to split a trap or step through it, and teach them how to avoid the trap before it can be set up. They must know how and when to stretch the trap or string it out with the dribble. These points will build recognition and instill confidence. Make your players realize that teams trap them as a sign of respect and because they fear their abilities! Use this positive approach to build up their confidence.

You can work on each of these offensive moves the same time you are working on trapping. Every time you teach defense, you should also be teaching offense. We mentioned before that it requires help from your assistant coaches, and this enables you to then work both sides of the ball at the same time. If your first unit is far superior to your second team, you might consider splitting up your team and equalizing their abilities, because you never know who might be in at the end of a game. You can run six offensive players against five defensive players or seven-on-five to give the weaker team a chance. But the more you practice, the better the second team will react to the first team's efforts and the better and more confidently your teams will handle pressure.

Change sides with the ball or pass diagonally when playing against double-teaming defenses, then follow your pass.

Things to remember to help your players handle pressure

1. The inbounder can run the baseline after a score.

2. The first pass gets the ball in and the second pass breaks the press.

3. If the trailer is necessary, he should trail at a 45-degree angle to provide a passing lane for the player with the ball.

4. Use flashing posts and attack pressure from behind.

5. A press breaker in the middle can pivot and go 360 degrees once he catches a pass.

6. Be alert. Teams usually press after a made free throw and teams press after timeouts, after scoring easy layups, when offensive men trail the ball handler, and when taking the ball out full-court on the baseline or sideline after a dead ball, substitution or timeout. Some teams pressure at midcourt following a made free throw and/or field goal. Be prepared.

7. Teach your players that the men without the ball must set up and create passing lanes for their teammates. It is their responsibility to get free. They can fake long and come back, or fake to the ball and circle long.

8. Cut to the ball to create a passing lane and outlet.

9. Look to score against the press. Make them pay.

10. Attack the press from behind.

11. Make the first outlet pass long, above the foul line, to immediately spread the defense. Don't pass to the near corner and invite the quick double-team.

12. You can pass to a teammate behind the baseline to inbound the ball, but only after a score.

13. We can screen and rescreen or look for the passer stepping in at a 45-degree angle after the inbound or baseline pass has been made.

14. When the point guard is denied the ball in the press offense, he must continue to cut and run his men off picks to try and get free.

15. To receive coming back to the ball, take your man toward midcourt and then come back.

16. To receive above the foul line, take your man to the baseline first and then break up court.

17. Break the press with the inbounder stepping in to receive the second pass or step another man behind the baseline to receive the pass and inbound the ball. The original inbounder should then cut to receive a pass. The inbounder can also break up the middle quickly after inbounding the ball.

18. You need to have a man posting in the middle versus the half court or three-quarter court trapping zone presses who force you sideline. Then you can diagonally turn and pass the ball ahead and run for a layup.

19. The weakside wing or post man should always fake long and flash to the middle as the press breaker in the press offense, especially when the offense is in trouble.

20. Catch the outlet pass with your back to the sideline. When you turn and look, you'll be able to see the whole court and all of the players. Avoid

reversing and dribbling immediately with your back to the court and getting called for an offensive foul because you didn't see the defense.

21. A man trapped on the low block or wing should pivot and also look to throw a skip pass to the far corner. The spotted up player might receive a screen from his weakside baseline post teammate on the defender rotating down on the weak side.

22. Look to change sides with the ball versus double-teaming. Go diagonally with the ball to take advantage of the farthest man from the ball being free.

23. Step back from the line when inbounding the ball. Give yourself a better passing angle and relieve defensive pressure.

Against pressing defenses, the first pass gets the ball in safely; the second pass breaks the press.

Rules for Attacking the Press

1. Don't stop and pick up your dribble immediately after you cross the mid-court line when advancing the ball vs. pressure. Stopping in this area invites double teaming the ball and using both the sideline and midcourt lines as additional defenders. Advance the ball between 5 and 10 feet over midcourt and away from the sideline before you stop and pick up your dribble.

2. Use the loop to split trapping defenders and open up the court and driving and passing lanes for the player being doubled.

3. Don't let the defense force you sideline and take away your options. Split midcourt and the sideline so you can dribble either way vs. pressure.

4. Possible outlets must establish passing lanes for the player being trapped.

5. Attack pressure from behind and flash to the middle vs. pressure. The middle man can then go 360 degrees with his pass.

6. Pass before the trap is formed, not once it engulfs you.

7. Baseline man on the weak side should come behind the press to attack it.

8. The point man must keep working to receive the ball when he is over played. He cannot stop moving after he is denied the ball the first time he tries to receive a pass.

9. Turn and face the defenders before dribbling, put them on the defensive.

10. The first big man downcourt should get behind the press and establish a passing lane to receive the ball.

Rules for Attacking the Press

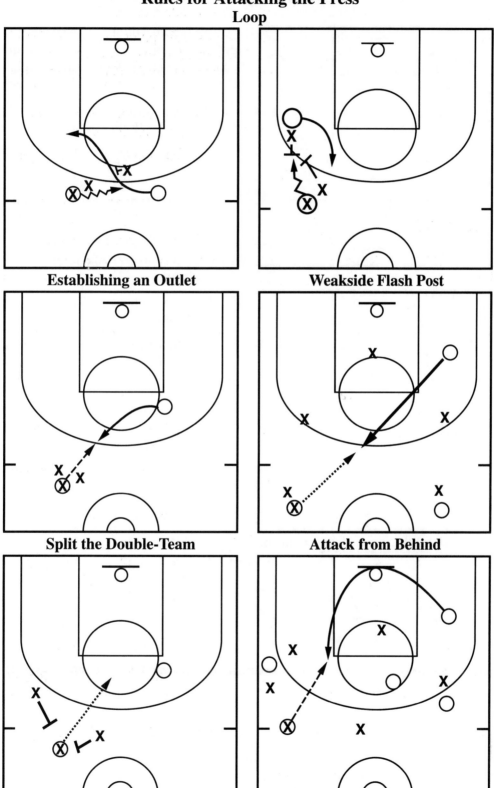

Loop

Establishing an Outlet

Weakside Flash Post

Split the Double-Team

Attack from Behind

Doubling the Post

(A)

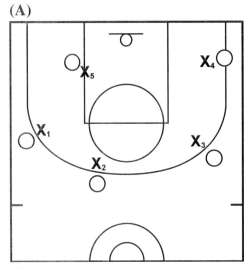

(B)

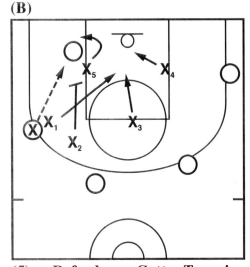

(5)   Defender on Cutter Trapping

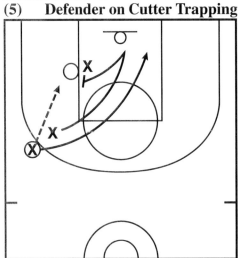

We practice doubling the post from either the 1, 2, 3 or 4 spots. Some coaches designate letters of the alphabet, colors or names to differentiate these spots.

A. Spots and numbers

B. Doubling from the 2 spot with other rotations. We want to zone off the ball with the players not trapping or doubling and we try to establish certain rules for trapping and doubling:

1. Turn the player being doubled back to his man.

2. Belly-up to the man being trapped with your hands up.

3. Don't permit the player being trapped to make a penetrating pass.

4. Force the trapped player to pass out over the trapper's outside shoulder.

5. If we trap off a cutter, we take the cutter below the ball and then come back to trap.

6. Players zoning off the ball cover the sideline, middle and basket or top, middle and basket (for a weakside rebound).

7. Many teams double with the nearest big man whether from the top or weak side, because he is more difficult to pass over, but the man he is guarding must be kept off the backboard.

8. We also trap on the pass, after one dribble or two dribbles.

Response to Double-Teaming Pressure

Use this drill for trapping and containing the dribbler defensively and offensively in order to teach the the dribbler how to respond to double-teaming pressure.

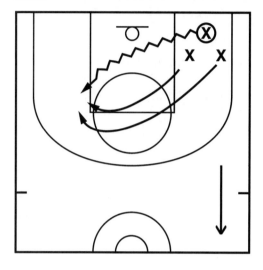

In this diagram, the player with the ball has 10 seconds to get the ball across midcourt. The defense must:

a. Contain him

b. Not foul

c. Keep him from beating them down the sideline

d. Make him pick up his dribble

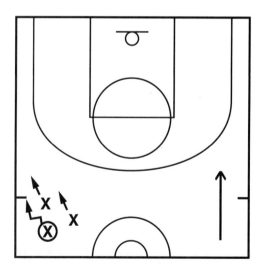

In this diagram, we run the same drill on the half court. Trap and contain the dribbler. You can put time on the shot clock. Move your feet. Don't bail the offensive player out by fouling him. Keep him down the sideline and stop penetration.

Special

Situations

Jump balls

You may only have one jump ball per game, but you should prepare for it. Try to make sure you don't give up an easy basket to start the game. Conversely, if you have an advantage on the jump, create a play which might result in an easy basket for you.

In the NBA, if the men jumping are even, most teams use the three-back rule. This means they have three players on the side of the court closest to the basket they are defending. They try not to give up an easy basket by being caught out of position.

You also want to teach the players where and how to tap the ball. Make sure it's tapped to the area where two of his teammates are side-by-side, even if it counteracts any set play. If there's no advantage around the circle, then coach your players to tap it to a specific corner and/or area and chase it down.

You should work with players on which hand to use when tapping the ball. Have them experiment jumping off each leg and extending each hand. Make them aware of the best combination and technique. Work on timing the jump to coincide with the toss. It all takes practice and your other players should all know the jumper's strong hand and where he prefers to tap the ball. It can mean extra possessions for a team. Execute jump balls whenever the opportunity arises in practice.

Photo©Frank McGrath

Jump Ball

Things to remember

1. Use three deep. Protect your goal.

2. Plan where your center goes after he taps. Should he sprint to the goal?

3. Tap to the corner (or a predesignated area) if you can't control the toss.

4. Tap between, over the heads and toward shirts of the same color.

5. Set up a play. Tap to one player and screen for another.

6. Alignment: We may also set up in a diamond or a box or even send a man deep.

Grab loose balls with two hands. Retain/ maintain possession first. Don't start to dribble before you have possession. The ball is precious.

Good clock management

Every player should know the time and score at any point in the game. With the shot clock, every player should be aware of how much time is remaining on it. To help players gain a "feel" for how much time is remaining on the shot clock, always use the shot clock in practice whenever you are running any kind of drills. Have a call from the sideline or on the court that cues the players when time is running down without tipping off the opposition. Many coaches overlook this and invariably are caught unaware in a crucial situation or point in the game. Don't permit your players to be caught napping. Attention to detail is of the utmost importance.

Also work on your one- or two-minute drills, both offensively and defensively. Use the game clock and scoreboard to set up particular situations. For example, you are three points up or down with a foul to give.

Players need to know how the time and score can dictate what plays are run, how quickly the plays develop and whether or not you want to take a 10-foot jumper or work for a three. They also have to be aware of what defense to run in given situations and must practice what to do in each instance.

With an eight-point lead with four minutes to go, you might want to milk the shot clock, depending on the flow of the game or you may decide to press to speed up the tempo. In either case, you should practice what strategy you intend or prefer to use.

Examples:

1. Down two points at home, 11 seconds left on the clock. Do you go for the win or drive the ball to the goal and penetrate? The defense does not want to foul, so you may get a layup, easy hoop and even a foul for a two- or three-point play. But don't give your opponent another opportunity to beat you.

2. Doubled in the frontcourt, no outlet. Do you throw a crosscourt pass, call timeout (what if there are no timeouts left?) or hold the ball for a jump ball and the opportunity to retain possession?

3. What do you do with the shot clock running down and the set play has broken down? Which man has the ball? Do you signal for a play or do you have an automatic to go to in this situation?

4. With 6.8 seconds left on a sideline out-of-bounds play. We have time to get a good shot and still not give opponents an opportunity to score. Utilize the clock. Know the score and tempo. Exercise good clock management.

5. With 15 seconds remaining in the game and up by 1, 2 or 3 points, don't trap. Lock in and play good defense. If down or tied with less than 15 seconds, look to trap and create a turnover.

When inbounding the ball, step back and away from the line to give yourself a better passing angle and view, and to relieve pressure.

Running a specific play

You might want to designate a special play for a specific player. You might always run it at a certain time in the game. You might have a special call or run it right out of a timeout. Some coaches like to use a specific play following a dunk by the opposition. Other coaches might want to have specific plays after a defender has picked up his fourth foul. There might also be a special play that has been set up beforehand for the end of the half or quarter. You also might want to have your players huddle up and call the next play before your opponent shoots his free throw. You can also huddle and call your defense before you shoot a free throw. But you must have practiced and reviewed each of these situations on a regular basis. Do this in practice when you scrimmage by having players huddle together to call a play before a free throw.

Special plays for use in a game can be predetermined and brought to the game on index cards to be used as a reference tool.

How to defend out-of-bounds plays

(Questions a coach must answer and things he should cover)

1. Establish where you want to channel the ball in all situations.

2. Protect the basket at all times.

3. On sideline out-of-bounds plays with less than five seconds, do you want to zone and trap?

4. Do you want to invert and switch everything when offensive players cross?

5. Should you pressure the passer with a bigger player?

6. Do you face-guard full court?

7. The man defending the inbounds passer should count five seconds to himself to know whether to step back and cover an outlet at four seconds to steal or more aggressively pressure the ball.

8. Don't bail opponents out on out-of-bounds plays. Don't foul with one second left on a five-seconds-to-inbound rule. Lock in and keep them in front of you.

Saving the ball

1. A play that comes up often in every game is saving the ball from going out of bounds. How many teams review that in practice? Spend part of a session or at least some time discussing and establishing basic principles. If the entire team knows what to do in that situation, you might gain an extra possession or two that could mean the difference between winning and losing a game. Most coaches preach to never save the ball and pass it directly under your opponent's basket, and this cannot be understated. However, there is more to it than that. You might want to designate a specific area of the court and tell your other players to look to go there when you save the ball. When your player is in midair, his teammates can get a jump on the opposition and have a better chance of recovering the ball, instead of possibly giving up the easy basket. Stress that move every time it comes up in a scrimmage until it becomes second nature for every player.

2. Have a plan for rebounds that can't be grabbed. Try to tap rebounds to the top of the circle or corner, for example, if your players get completely boxed out. Rather than standing around, condition them to be alert to field and recover a possible tap to a prestated area where they know a teammate might tip the ball if he can't grab the rebound. You want to gain possession of the ball any way you can. Little things win ballgames and ball possession is the key commodity.

Try to tap rebounds or loose balls to predesignated areas of the court.

Special Situations

A. On a Last Shot in the Quarter (LSQ) situation the players on the floor must know when to run the play. We don't want to start too soon, because we don't want our opponents to get the last shot. We also want to give ourselves the opportunity to rebound and put back a missed shot.

B. Sideline out of bounds, five seconds left, end of game, down by one, two or three points. Do you:
    a. Pressure the pass or lay off and play in the middle for a steal?
    b. Pressure inbounder for three seconds and step back into the passing lanes?
    c. Face guard?
    d. Invert and switch every cross?
    e. Look for a steal?
    f. Foul immediately?
    g. Channel the pass to a specific area and trap!

C. End of the quarter, 23 seconds left, you are up six or seven points, your team is shooting a free throw and you feel your opponent will hold the ball for the final shot of the quarter. Do you press full court after a made free throw, trying to cause a turnover and using up some clock or do you fall back and defend the last shot?

D. The point man has the responsibility to and must call a play and give a verbal or hand signal if eight seconds or less are on the shot clock and the play has broken down. This must be predetermined and practiced daily. It can be a specific play or movement into your motion or passing game. If a play breaks down, our players look to cut and screen someone else, especially the point guard if he has the ball. We also have our players screen for someone on the reversal of the ball.

E. In the NBA, a two-for-one situation exists if we have the ball with around 38 seconds or less on the game clock at the end of a quarter or game. We want to get a quick shot so that we'll have another opportunity to score once our opponent has taken his last shot. We run a predetermined play in all two-for-one situations and practice and review them almost every day and especially during our game day shoot-arounds and meetings.

F. Have a special verbal signal on offense and defense to alert all the players that the shot clock is running down.

G. Have a predetermined signal to let your players know that you want to foul to stop the clock.

H. LSG, three seconds on the game clock, no time outs left and your team is down by one point. You have the ball in the front court, either under the basket or on the sideline. Have you prepared for the eventuality and do your players know exactly what play to run?

I. No timeouts, down one point, five seconds to go and your opponents are shooting a free throw. Have you practiced what you want to do in this situation?

J. What about taking the ball out from three-quarter court in the same situation with no time outs?

K. You are down by three points with one second to go. You are shooting two free throws. If you make the first and now are two points down, have you practiced how you want to miss the shot and where you should rebound it to put it back in and tie the score?

L. Your opponent has the ball out in the corner with three seconds to go on the shot clock. How are you going to defend them? Zone, man-to-man, trap or straight up?

Rules for Defending Out-of-Bounds Plays

1. Man-to-man defense

2. Zone defense

3. Switch everything every time players cross, screen across, etc.

4. Stay with your man. Deny and don't let him receive the ball.

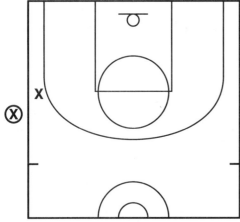

Protect the inside; force the pass to the outside.

5. Invert and switch every cross. (Taller defenders closer to the goal, shorter defenders on the perimeter.)

6. Protect the goal when defending the inbounds passer. Hands up. Force the pass out and away from the goal.

7. Channel and pressure all passes out, not inside.

8. Pressure the inbounds passer with a taller player.

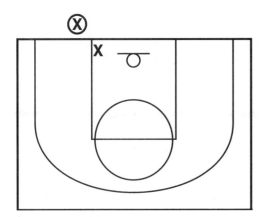

Protect the inside and the basket.

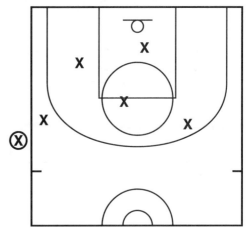

Sideline out-of-bounds zone defense.

Rules for Defending Out-of-Bounds Plays

9. Don't pressure the passer. Play the passing lanes and look for the steal.

10. Do you want to think about trapping the first pass if it goes to the corner?

11. Special defenses for short clock situations.

12. Switch off the inbounds passer if a cutter goes by. Sideline out of bounds and baseline out of bounds.

13. Substitute stronger rebounders and better defenders when you need a big play.

14. If the pass goes inside, zone trap. If the pass goes outside, match up man-to-man.

15. Be aware of the inbounds passer stepping in, cutting, screening or getting a screen. The passer is a definite threat. Body check him and deny him the ball.

16. Face guard with your back to the ball with the defender on the passer pressuring the ball and yelling "ball" once the pass is released so he can alert his teammates that the dribble is dead and they can deny and pressure their men.

Sideline Out-of-Bounds 1-3-1 Zone Defense

Try to force the ball to the corner. If the first pass is outside, match up man-to-man. If the first pass goes to the corner, trap. If the first pass goes to the middle man, go man-to-man, but slough down on him from the outside.

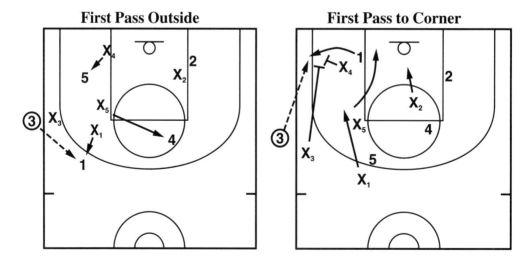

| First Pass Outside | First Pass to Corner |

The two-minute drill and last-second situations

Practice your one- or two-minute offenses with the game clock as often as possible. Go over specific situations that may come up in a game:

■ Ahead by one with 30 seconds to play; behind by one with 15 seconds to go. If you are on offense, do you want to take an easy shot or play keep away? Whom do you want to handle the ball? When should you call a time out? If you are on defense, do you want to go for a steal or commit a quick foul? Whom do you foul? Know if you are shooting the bonus on the next foul. How many timeouts does each team have left?

■ What do you do on offense or defense with the score tied and less than 20 seconds on the clock? Quickly foul the poorest free-throw shooter if he touches the ball or defend until the buzzer sounds?

Your team must know: 1) when to drive; 2) when to shoot the three; 3) when to foul; 4) when to play for a stop; 5) when to play for a tie; or 6) when to play for the win. Offensively, you may want to penetrate and get to the basket quickly knowing that most defenders are afraid to foul in these situations. Know what to do when a play breaks down. A good rule is to have players away from the ball look to screen for one another and to have the nearest man to the ball screen the ball for a screen-and-roll opportunity.

Proper clock management

You need to practice last-second situations, both offensively and defensively. You may or may not have timeouts available, so you need to have preset plays your players can rely on in each of these instances. Practice them often with the game clock and scoreboard. Players should feel comfortable knowing where to look to get that information. It's another small advantage for the home team. They must know when to penetrate (time on the clock) to give you time to score and to eliminate the opponent's ability to take the last shot. You should practice your stall or delay game tactics so your players know how to milk the clock and/ or play keep-away. Know what defenses you want to play to get the ball back quickly.

Players must also be aware of last-second situations on the shot clock and a 2-for-1 opportunity with the shot clock. You have to be able to get into the play from both a rebound or made basket. You should have a play for sideline out of bounds or baseline out of bounds with few seconds on the game or shot clock and no timeouts available.

Practice time needs to be set aside on a regular basis to cover and review all of the following last-second situations: Inbounding from half court, three-quarter court, full court, on out-of-bounds plays, from any place on the court with varying amounts of time remaining in the game.

Foul problems

If an opposing player picks up his second foul early in the first half, you might want to be ready to run a play right at that player. If he picks up his fourth (fifth in the NBA) in the second half, you might go right at the player to make him defend or see if he would rather not put himself in jeopardy by fouling and therefore will play soft defense.

Take advantage of the team foul situation, too. If you get into the bonus early, drive the ball to the basket. Get to the free-throw line as much as possible. Make sure you emphasize the importance of high percentage free-throw shooting to your team and devote practice time to free-throw shooting every day.

Make your players conscious of not committing quick second or third fouls. Silly or inadvertent fouls could put them on the bench unnecessarily.

We also don't want to put teams in the bonus early and don't want to commit offensive fouls and lose the ball or give offensive rebounds in crucial situations.

Fouling to stop the clock

Establish rules and principles on when to foul and whom to foul in a given situation. Don't wait until the final minute of a game to decide whether or not it is in your favor to foul by searching for an opponent's statistics sheet. Know before the game whom you want to foul and make sure your players know which players are poor free-throw shooters. Foul hard when necessary to be certain not to give up three-point plays. Prevent the basket and make the player have to convert two free throws, not a basket and one free throw. But don't make it an obvious intentional foul.

Do you have both a verbal and nonverbal signal to alert players that you want to commit a foul to stop the clock? It cannot be an obvious signal that would make the referee call a deliberate, intentional or flagrant foul. Try to disguise your signal and the way you commit the foul.

Don't waste time chasing players, trying to foul them. Coach your players on how to foul quickly. Stop the clock! In certain situations, it's more important for a player to commit his fifth foul (6th in the NBA) to stop the clock, even though he'll be disqualified from the game. In the final seconds of a tight game, proper clock management may be just as important as which players you have in the game. Give yourself and your team every opportunity to win the game.

Substituting

Players must know their roles. Players on the bench should know whom they normally replace and when they usually enter the game. They should know who that man is guarding and should be studying that player's moves on both ends of the floor. Know the personal foul situations.

Prepare your players for situation substituting in the closing minutes, using your top defensive players when the other team has the ball and putting in your best shooters, free-throw shooters and ball handlers when you have the ball.

Coaches should develop a substitution pattern whenever possible. It helps the starters know when they will be getting a break and it helps the substitutes know when they should be getting mentally and physically ready (by stretching) to enter the game. There are two major advantages to using your bench:

1. You can keep your starters fresh by playing them less minutes.
2. You can develop the players on the bench by giving them more minutes in the game in case you are beset with foul trouble or injuries.

Some coaches try to get all their possible substitutes they are thinking of using into the game in the first half so if they need them in the second half, they won't be going in cold in a crucial situation without any feel for the game. Plan ahead and be prepared for whatever might possibly occur.

Utilizing your timeouts

Should you save your timeouts for the end of the game or use them early to stop the other team's momentum or to put in a special play? Should you use timeouts to rest players or should you just substitute for them on a dead ball? This is an individual coach's preference.

Some coaches adhere to a principle of never wanting to call the first timeout of a game. They construe it as a sign of admitting weakness. Others hesitate to call timeouts on offense at the end of a game because they are afraid to give the opposing coach an opportunity to adjust. Again, it is individual preference that dictates your decision.

When should you call timeouts in the closing seconds of a tight game? Should you call a timeout to freeze a free-throw shooter?

Whenever you call a timeout, always have a purpose and make sure everyone in the huddle understands the message you want to get across. If there are media or automatic timeouts, know when they are going to occur. Don't waste a timeout if the officials will be calling one on the next dead ball. But don't take this so literally that you watch an eight-point lead disappear in 45 seconds while you wait for the officials to call their timeout.

Once you've called a timeout, what do you say?

If you just want to give your players a breather, keep it upbeat and simple. If you want to settle your team down, exude confidence. If you are unhappy, show it. A lot of coaches feel that you shouldn't cover more than three things in any timeout. It's believed that players won't be focused on more than three things. Make sure everyone knows and understands anything you've diagrammed. Don't assume they do. Ask questions to be certain they understand.

You might use timeouts to make a substitution, but remember timeouts are precious! If your star player has gotten into foul trouble early or a player is slightly injured, you might not want to chance it that a dead ball will occur before you can get him back in the game and take advantage of the situation.

Be consistent in how you approach timeouts. If you want to discuss the situation with your assistant coaches, then do that for the first 20 seconds or so. Let the players rest and get a drink. Then be clear and concise in your instructions so that everyone in the huddle — not just the five players in the game — can hear you. Make sure you cover everything you want. If not, late in a tight game, you might want to call a second straight timeout. Ask if there are any questions. Then quickly review everything you've said once again before the team leaves the bench.

Some coaches like to draw up new plays during a timeout. Others prefer to have enough plays so that you can run something that you have worked on. You might want to diagram a slight variation of a particular play, instead of diagramming an entirely new play. Do what works for you and what makes you and your players most comfortable. Coaches have been known to bring cards to the game with diagrams of special situation plays they might want to use.

You also should anticipate any substitutions or changes your opponent might make during the timeout or have an assistant or trainer watch the opponent's huddle to alert you to any personnel changes they might make so you too can make the proper substitutions and matchups.

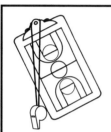 In timeouts, diagram your plays so you can be sure every player knows his assignment and understands what you are trying to get the team to execute.

Taking advantage of an opponent's individual weaknesses

There are several ways to take advantage of an opponent's weaknesses. You might want to run plays right at their leading scorer so he has to work harder on defense than he's accustomed. It might tire him out or get him into foul trouble. You might also break a shooter's concentration if you run out on him and foul him the first time he has the ball. He'll know you'll be there the rest of the night. Perhaps play three or four different defenders on him so that his normal rhythm will be affected. Trap him as soon as he receives the ball. Do anything you need to do to help you win the game and make the rules work for your team. If you are playing a poor outside shooting team, you might want to utilize a zone defense.

You should also recognize any mismatches on the floor. Mismatches aren't created just by one player being taller than another. The mismatch might be in quickness or in experience. The job you do scouting the opposition will dictate how well you can take advantage of the other team's weaknesses. Utilize your scouts and their reports. Communicate with them and find out anything they feel that can help you win.

Using the shot and game clocks in practice

Use them every time you scrimmage. Players need to get used to looking at the score and the clocks. Some coaches use the clock in all drills to emphasize its importance to their players. Remember, controlling or establishing tempo, and knowing the time and score are of the utmost importance if you want your team to be successful.

Game
Preparations

Pregame routines

Prior to a game, assign and explain everyone's role. Talk about the matchups and make the defensive assignments. Use the blackboard to list the keys to winning, key defensive assignments or certain plays that the opponents run or that you have put in for this game. List the goals that you have for that game and review any short-term goals you might have. You might have a scout video running of the other team or a video of your most recent success while the players are dressing. Use the blackboard to diagram plays your opponents like to run and discuss and review your defensive strategy designed to stop these plays.

Involve your assistants in pregame preparations. Assign each coach a specific responsibility and hold him accountable for presenting it to the team. How and whom do you want to handle shoot-arounds and walk-throughs?

Scouting to take away a team's tendencies

First, you have to decide if you believe in scouting and if you scout the opposition, how detailed you want the report to be. When do you want to see the opponent (right before they play you)? How many times do you want to see them? The two most recent games prior to your contest with them? You should find out what style they play, who their best players are and what tendencies they usually exhibit. Who are their key players and who do they go to in crunch time? What play do they run in crunch time? What are their need plays? How and if you can change the tempo against them? You'll want to know who are their strong defenders, rebounders, shooters and ball handlers. You'll also want to know who are their poorest defenders, rebounders, shooters and ball handlers. If possible, you want to know their signals or calls for specific plays or situations. These are an individual coach's preference. Your point guard can help during a game by repeating their calls and by relaying them to you and your players. Discuss changes in strategy at halftime or during timeouts.

As a coach you have to anticipate your opponent's tactics and game plan. You have to anticipate how they will play against a team with your philosophy. How are they going to stop you from doing what you want to do? You have to anticipate that and prepare your players for each situation during your practices, as well as during the game. Know your opponent's tendencies, frequencies and most effective and efficient plays. Develop a key agenda of five or six things you want to concentrate on as the keys to victory on a given night against a given opponent. Have your players focused and aware of your game preparation and emphasis.

- If you play a team more than once, you must be sure to recognize new plays, changed calls or signals to update your report or game plan.

- Check previous scouting and game reports for opponents' tendencies. Utilize every resource at your disposal.

- Get your players to help you with the opposing team's signals or play calls. Have them relay them to you during free throws or timeouts. Every bit of information you can gather will help you win and be successful.

- Utilize videos as much as possible. You need offensive and defensive tapes of your opponents. Break down tapes of your opponents' most frequently used plays plays, both half-court and out-of-bounds.

We remind our players that the first four minutes and last four minutes of every period (for an NBA 12-minute quarter) are the most crucial minutes of every game and concentration is of the utmost importance at these times. In college, the first five or six and last five or six minutes of each half are the most critical and intense times where your team must be completely focused and determined.

I can't play everybody, but I am obligated to coach every one of my players every day.

Sample Scouting Form

Date _____

Score _____

vs _____ at _____

Officials _____

Match-Ups
Home

_____

P.G.	_____		P.G.	_____
S.G.	_____		S.G.	_____
S.F.	_____		S.F.	_____
P.F.	_____		P.F.	_____
C.	_____		C.	_____

3-Point Shooters

1. _____
2. _____
3. _____
4. _____
5. _____

Defense: Pick & Roll

_____

_____

Defense: Post

_____

_____

Dbl Team

_____

_____

Starters

1. _____
2. _____
3. _____
4. _____
5. _____

Poor Foul Shooters

1. _____
2. _____
3. _____
4. _____
5 _____

_____

_____

_____

_____

Best Foul Shooters

1. _____ 3. _____
2. _____ 4. _____

Subs

1. _____
2. _____
3. _____
4. _____
5 _____

Sample Scouting Form
(Indicate number of times each play is used)

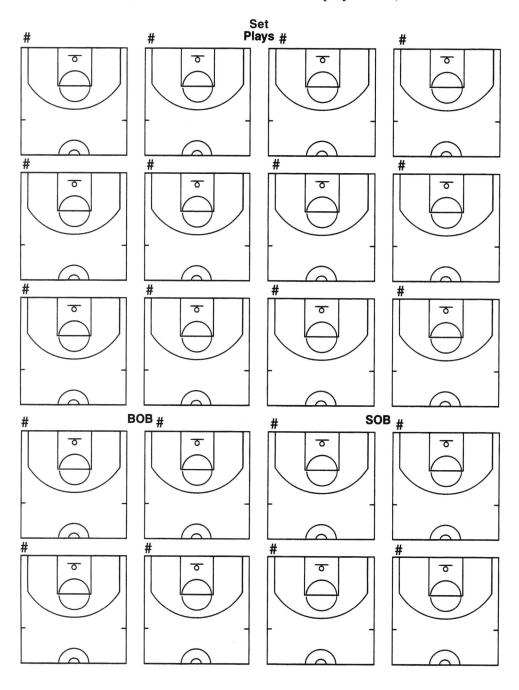

Sample Scouting Form

DEFENSE

DATE _____

1st Half
Home   Opp.

Steals			Steals
Blocks			Blocks
2nd Shots			2nd Shots

2nd Half
Home   Opp.

Steals			Steals
Blocks			Blocks
2nd Shots			2nd Shots

Final
Home   Opp.

Steals			Steals
Blocks			Blocks
2nd Shots			2nd Shots

OPPONENT PLAYS

1. _____
2. _____
3. _____
4. _____
5. _____
6. _____
7. _____
8. _____
9. _____
10. _____
11. _____
12. _____

GAME COMMENTS

_____
_____
_____
_____
_____
_____
_____
_____
_____
_____
_____
_____
_____
_____
_____
_____

Sample Scouting Form
Plays

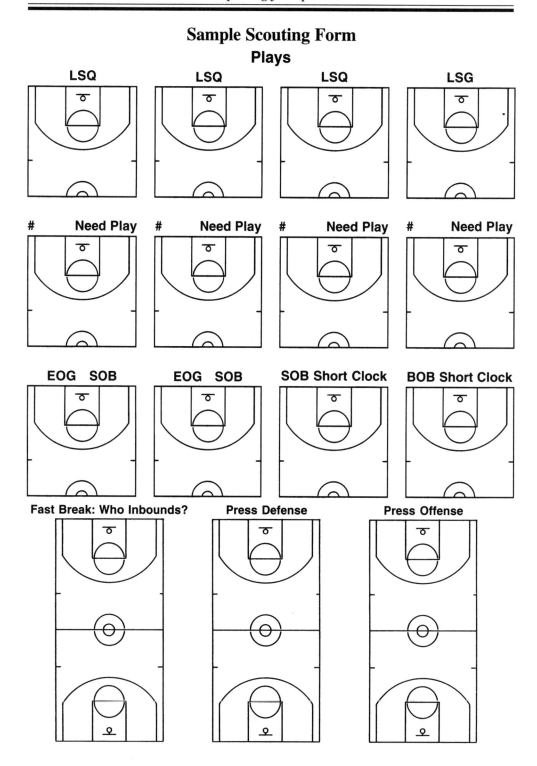

 # Summary

An important thing every coach should remember is that very few coaches receive a great deal of compensation for the job they do. Because of that, it's important that a coach enjoys what he is doing and that he also makes the experience enjoyable for his players.

The easiest way to make it enjoyable for the players is to work every day at helping them become better individual players. It's important that your players develop a joy and enthusiasm for playing the game. If a coach truly loves the game, he then will be able to transfer this feeling to the players. Coaching isn't a job, it's a labor of love. When you see the growth in a player or a group of players, you realize what coaching is all about. All of the agony, the ecstasy and the long hours of hard work definitely make it all worthwhile. You have put a group of players together and created a team that works as one unit. When everything blends together, it's tremendously rewarding.

When a team wins, the credit should go to the players. If you're in coaching to satisfy your ego, you're in it for the wrong reasons. The game belongs to the players. They're the ones who are out there participating. You may have greater knowledge and experience than the players, but in reality you're just contributing to the development of their skills and love for the game. You have to deal with players as people and understand that they are human beings, not a means for you to get ahead professionally. Hopefully, when your players get older, they'll still love to play, even if it's three-on-three, in an industrial league or maybe just on a hoop in the backyard.

When a team wins, the credit should go to the players.

Photo©Frank McGrath

You have to treat players fairly and consistently. Every player should be treated with dignity and respect. That means players 1 through 12. You should require effort and recognize it in every player. If a player has a particular skill, nurture it and try to maximize it.

Every coach will experience a lot of ups and downs. You must have a sense of humor as well as being careful not to overcoach. You can't be tense or make your players tense. You have to always maintain your poise, confidence and composure. Remember, whether you win or lose a particular game is not the most important thing in life. What's important is that your players feel a sense of accomplishment. They should feel good about their sacrifices, their dedication and their experiences, not only their won-loss record.

We can all be teachers, communicators, father figures, motivators, disciplinarians and psychologists, and still strive for perfection. Set an example for your players. If you want your players to be on time, you need to be on time. If you want your players to dress appropriately, you need to dress appropriately. If you want them to respect other people, then you need to respect other people. You have to be organized and a step ahead of the opposition. You have to prepare your players for every possible development, and you need to be strong enough to accept responsibility and criticism when it is warranted. You must also be strong enough to admit your mistakes.

You have to develop a sense of team. No man is a mountain, and the only way we get things done is by working together. It starts with the ticket taker in the gym and goes to the janitor, the equipment man, the secretary, the school nurse, the booster club, the bus driver, the parents, the student body and fans. You must acknowledge and recognize everyone associated with the team. You should do whatever you can do for them. Make them all feel part of the program. If you do that, they'll want to see you succeed and they will help you succeed.

Every coach is different. One might concentrate on offense, another on defense, another on discipline. However, coaching is really an extension of your personality. You have to teach what works for you, not what works for Phil Jackson, Dean Smith or Bob Knight or any other coach who has been successful over a period of time. You have to realize that we all make mistakes. Maybe you can pick up one or two things from attending a clinic, a camp, a game or a team's practice that you can adapt to your philosophy. You still must be yourself, however. You should adjust your philosophy to your personnel and its level of competition. You can't just copy people. Don't emulate style if it's not your style. You might incorporate a particular play if you think it will work in your specific situation, but don't try to be someone else. Great coaches never stop learning, they just continue studying and analyzing the game and building lifelong relationships with their players and the folks they work with.

Remember, you live with your players for a long season. They can't fool you, and you can't fool them. You need to set goals every day, goals the team and individuals are able to accomplish. You have to strive to motivate them to get better and improve every day.

Hopefully, this book will show you that there are different ways to coach and different ways to play. There's no better feeling than seeing basketball become a training ground and foundation for what your players will accomplish the rest of their lives. More importantly, we hope that we have been able to share and demonstrate our love for the game with you.

Glossary of

Key Terms

Some teams use different terms or symbols to describe a specific maneuver. This is probably due to a desire to confuse opponents and to stay away from being stereotyped. When appropriate, we will try to give two or three interpretations.

Ahead: Action when the ball is passed from the wing to the corner in early offense or transition from offense to defense.

ATO: An acronym for After a Timeout.

ATW: An acronym for All The Way. Describes running a play through from the start to the finish; running all the options before shooting.

Belly-up: A defensive man making contact with his body forcing the post man with the ball toward the trapping defender instead of reversing the ball to an open spot.

Blast: Diagonal Hawk cut from high to low post on the strong side offensively.

Blind Pig: Weakside flash post or pinch post when the wing is overplayed to set up a wing backdoor move to the basket.

Blitz the pick-and-roll: The screener's defender traps the dribbler as the defender on the dribbler chases and gets over the screen to double-team the dribbler and stop penetration. Also called by a color, letter, etc.

BOB: An acronym for Baseline Out of Bounds.

Box set: An offensive alignment when the four offensive players without the ball are positioned in a box or square, approximately 15-17 feet apart.

Bump/Chuck/Body: The defender makes contact with the offensive man without the ball to slow up, stop or impede his cut. It can be used against cutters and screeners.

Bump back: Screen and come back to the ball after the offensive player has used your screen. Keep the defender on your back.

Bury: When a guard passing to the wing cuts in front of the wing to the strongside corner.

Buttonhook: Fake a screen across the lane, quickly stop and come back to the ball, sealing your defender on your back.

Center field: Area above the circle or three-point line in the middle of the court in the offensive end where an offensive player is positioned to receive an outlet pass in case players are in trouble in a position to reverse the ball and also for defensive balance.

Chase: Can be action where the low post goes across the lane in the same direction as the dribbler in a high pick-and-roll. It can also be action where a shooter on the baseline uses a staggered screen to come up to the ball.

Cherry pick: The defender on a jump shooter contesting a shot and taking off for the offensive end of the court for an easy basket after a rebound or to disconcert the shooter.

Circle: Having a post man without the ball circle up or down the lane to the ball, creating a passing lane for the offensive post man being doubled by his defender. Also can be referred to as curling to establish a passing lane.

Corner: The area of the court where the baseline and sideline come together.

Cross: Action where two offensive players run from one side of the court to the other with or without screening for one another, but forcing their defenders to follow them.

Counter: Action of an offensive player coming up from the baseline or going over an offensive screener to the weak side, utilizing a backscreen to free himself from his defender. Also called a flare.

Curl: Running a man from the weak to the strong side of the court off a low-post player, but after coming off the screen, the cutter immediately curves or curls around the screen in an effort to lose his man and/or free the screener.

DHO: An acronym for Dribble Handoff between two players.

Diagonal: A cut from the weak side to the strong side with or without a screen.

Direct: A pass from the point to an offensive player on or above the elbow who then makes a straight pass into the same side low post. Also called drop.

Double: A two-man shoulder-to-shoulder baseline or other two-man screen.

Drag: A high pick-and-roll run with the point and a big man across the middle of the court.

Drive and kick: The player with the ball penetrating causing the defensive players to converge on him to stop his drive, leaving other offensive players to receive a pass from him in scoring position. Also referred to as "penetrate and pitch."

Drop: A direct post-up pass from the strongside wing or elbow.

Duck in: The low-post man stepping into the defensive player and up to the ball to receive a pass from the high post or wing. An attempt to seal the defender on your back.

Elbow: The spot parallel or a step below or above the foul line and outside the free-throw lane where a man can post up with his back to the basket.

EOG: An acronym for End-of-the-Game play.

FC: Full court.

Fist: Can be a signal for the pick-and-roll, post up or double stack action offensively. Also used defensively to signal a type of trap. We can add up, down, out, right or left to fist or any other call to denote a special play.

Fist to palm: A signal often used to indicate a direct post up on the block.

Flat: Offensive set where the four players without the ball spread out across the baseline. (1-4 baseline set)

Flex: Horizontal baseline cut over or under a post man, away from the ball, to the ball side. Usually run through the free-throw lane.

Floppy: Wings crossing off baseline screens in scissors action.

Get: Pass, follow and get the ball handed back to you.

Go: Dribble drive the ball from one side to the other on a high pick-and-roll maneuver.

G to F: Acronym for Guard to Forward, usually denotes a pass, moving the ball closer to the basket, rather than away.

G to G: Acronym for Guard to Guard, usually denotes a horizontal pass, moving the ball from one side of the court to the other.

Guard to forward: Penetrating pass from the top to the wing area on the same side.

Guard to guard: Horizontal pass from one player to the other across the court.

Hand check: Defensive act of forcing or controlling and channeling the dribbler or post man in the direction you want him to go. In the NBA, the defender must use his forearm, rather than the palm of his hand to avoid being called for a personal foul.

Hawk cut: A diagonal cut off the high post from the weak side to the ballside post area. Example: from weakside elbow to strongside block.

HC: Half Court.

Head hunt: Screen the defense in the numbers. Establish position for contact.

H.O.: An acronym for Hand Off.

Hold: An offensive player fakes a cut and maintains his position or posts his man on the low block.

Horns: Usually describes a horizontal screen across the lane by a small man to screen a big man. It can also be used to describe a pick-and-roll play.

Ice/ISO: Isolating a man with the ball by clearing other defenders away from the ball, permitting an offensive player to go one-on-one.

Lift: Posting in "direct" action, the two offensive players not in the play step out on the weak side above the three-point line where their defenders must follow them instead of helping.

Lob: A pass to a post man when he has sealed his defender from the basket. The pass usually is aimed toward the front of the rim.

Lock and lob: High-low action when the low post is fronted. The post man turns and seals the defender on his back as the wing passes to him or to the foul line area where a lob pass is thrown to the low-post player by the man at the high post.

Lock in: Defending good shooters and not helping or rotating off them in a trapping or doubling team defense. We "marry" the shooter.

Loop: Maneuver to break pressure by having an offensive man without the ball split the two defenders laterally to open up a clear side for the dribbler or provide a throwback option for the dribbler if the two defenders try to trap him. Also called a "split."

LSQ: An acronym for Last Shot in the Quarter.

Marry: Completely deny good shooters the basketball. Do not help when he does not have the ball and is in a good position to shoot.

Misdirection: A screen set by the offensive man farthest away from the ball for the player nearest the ball.

Mismatch: Situation where a taller player is being defended by a smaller or weaker player.

Misses/Makes: The results of an offensive play. Many teams fast break on misses only and not when the opponents make or score a basket.

Motion: Structured free-lance offensive scheme where five men are passing, cutting and screening for one another and reversing the ball to create easy baskets off movement. All cuts are predicated by reading the defense so the offense can counter the defense's moves.

Multiply: Action by which the team that has just scored a layup or breakaway basket off a steal immediately regroups defensively and pressures full court to create havoc and another immediate scoring opportunity.

Need/Crunch: A play used by a team when it must have a basket, usually at the end of a game or in a crucial situation.

One & done: The act of trying to trap the ball once in a full- or half-court press. Once the pass is made out of the trap or if the trap is unsuccessful, the defense retreats and plays its usual defense.

Open: Similar to motion. Passing game action without a post man.

Penetrate-and-pitch: The act of the dribbler driving to the goal and, if stopped, passing to a teammate spotted up in a position to shoot.

Pick-the-Picker: Action where a screen is set in offensive action for the player setting the first screen.

Pinch Post (PP): Area outside the elbow where a posting player can set up to almost isolate his defender. May be on the weak or strong side.

Pin down: A screen from high to low where the high man goes and screens the low man's defender. It can be diagonal or vertical.

Pistol: Another signal to designate a special play.

Pop: Offensive players faking inside and popping to the ball.

Power: Banging the ball into the post.

Reverse pivot: Catching the ball and spinning back to the goal to the outside, away from your defender.

Ride high: Bump and body the cutter over the screen in the direction you wish to force him.

Rip: A backpick, usually a small man on a big man from low to high.

Rip blast: Hawk or UCLA cut with return backpick to free the shooter or post a big man. Rip signal for this type of backpick could be a raised fist.

Roll: The screener diving to the goal with the defender on his back after setting a screen and having the dribbler pass the ball to him.

Rub: Cutting a player from the weak side to the strong side. Similar to slice.

Run and jump: A defender in front of the ball leaves his man and tries to trap the dribbler from the front or make him give up the ball.

Scissors: Crossing two men (wings) off low-post men with the ball at the point or where one player passes to the post and cuts above the post man and then another post man cuts off the cutter and splits the post.

Screen across: Set by an offensive man nearest to the ball for a man parallel to him and away from the ball. Also known as a lateral screen or horizontal screen.

Shoot the gap: Step inside and slide through a downscreen to steal the pass.

Shuffle: High to low cut to the ball after a pass from the strong to weak side, usually diagonally high or low, rubbing your man off a post man.

Sideline: A defensive tactic where instead of blitzing the pick-and-roll, the defense forces the dribbler to the sideline, prohibiting him from turning the corner.

Single: A solitary baseline screen.

Skip pass: A cross-court pass over the weakside defense from one side to the other.

Slice: Weakside flat cut from the wing as the ball moves around the perimeter, using a single or double screen.

Slippage: Description of why a play broke down.

Slip the pick (defensively): Moving inside the screener toward the ball, not letting him make contact with you when he attempts to set a vertical screen.

Slip the pick (offensively): Pick-and-roll action where the screener's defender is above his outside shoulder and near the ball. The offensive player recognizes this and dives to the goal instead of looking to set a screen.

SOB: An acronym for Sideline Out of Bounds.

Spot up/Space out: Areas where shooters go to wait for the ball by establishing passing lanes when the ball is on the low post and the defense may be double-teaming or trapping.

Squeeze: In pick-and-roll defense where the defender on the screener "hugs" his man to permit the defender on the dribbler to go under the screener and his defender. It is often used when the dribbler is not a good jump shooter. The squeeze also can be used to combat a screen off the ball to help the defense go under both the screener and defender.

Staggered: Double or triple screens for a shooter. Not shoulder to shoulder, but successive.

Step back: On a screen or pick-and-roll, where the screener steps back once the dribbler has passed, instead of rolling to the goal.

Step in: Action where an offensive player sets a screen and steps to the ball or where a post player steps into the lane, seals his defender and looks for a pass from a teammate.

Step up: Action where a low post offensive player comes up from the baseline to screen a defensive wing playing the ball. It sets up pick-and-roll action. It can be used in the middle of the court as well, for high pick-and-rolls and also in transition in your early offense if the dribbler is being pressured. It also can be used in transition in the frontcourt where a blind screen is set for the dribbler.

Stops: Act where a defensive team prohibits the offense from scoring on a given possession.

Stretch or string out: An attempt by a dribbler being blitzed in a pick-and-roll to dribble out and to the other side of the court, forcing the high trap man to follow him.

Swing: Passing the ball from one side of the court to the other through the high-post area. Also called reversing or changing sides with the ball.

Switch: On defense, when offensive players cross with or without the ball, the two defenders coming together trade and take each other's man.

Tandem: Fast-break defense where one player is in front of the other in a straight line from the basket.

Throw back: Dribbling and penetrating from one side to the other, moving the defense and passing back to the weak side to a teammate who has screened or looped for you.

Thru: A guard passing to the wing and cutting to the weak side of the court.

Thumb: It can signal turnout action, post-up call or other maneuver.

Tighten out: When a defensive player releases and runs to the other end of the court when the man he is playing shoots a jump shot. Also called cherry picking or leaking out.

Top of the head (patting): A signal that might indicate a blind step-up pick-and-roll on the wing in transition or any other special offensive maneuver.

Trap: Two defenders doubling the man with the ball in any area of the court.

Triangle: Play with three offensive players set up in this configuration.

Turnout/Turn: Running a man from the weak to strong side of the court off a low-post player.

Twirl: Signal to describe desired offensive action.

Twist: Moving from side to side on the offensive end. Also called a twirl.

Two-for-one: Offensive team's desire to score quickly with between 30-40 seconds remaining in a quarter so that it ensures itself of two scoring opportunities to its opponent's one.

Two-man game: Offensive pick-and-roll between two players or other play involving just two offensive players, usually isolated from the other players on the court.

UCLA: A passer's cut from the top of the high post to the baseline after he has passed to the wing on the ball side.

Upblock: A screen between two offensive players without the ball where the lower offensive player screens the defender of the higher player. Also known as a backpick.

Up the line: Defenders switch off their men and up to the next man when defending multiple screens or staggered screens.

Utah cut: The reverse of the Hawk cut, whereby a baseline offensive player on the ball side sets a diagonal back screen for a high-post man or receives a diagonal downscreen from the high-post man. It is named after the team that began using this play most frequently.

Wing: The player or area on either sideline below the point man. Attempt to set triangles.

Zipper: A small low-post player waiting for a vertical downscreen from a high-post player and using the screen to come high to the ball.